You're Gonna Know Me, puts the power of self-promotion your career directly into the hands of you the actor. Becoming an Actor is hard work, so give yourself the edge. This direct, enthusiastic guide for actors teaches you how to promote yourself and succeed. A professional actor is a business. To be successful you must understand how to develop and promote yourself. In this book you will learn how to utilize promotional tools and strategies to gain the winning edge.

You're Gonna Know Me will help you take control of the business side of your creative career. By acknowledging that self-promotion is vital to an actor's livelihood you can have a better chance at success. This book is a guide to using many of those promotional tools and techniques that the actor can easily master for their own self-promotion.

In *You're Gonna Know Me*, Ron Cooper helps actors and others in the arts understand the power of branding. This guide walks the reader through the process of creating a personal brand and promoting it through every step of the process.

Ron Cooper is a renowned authority on brand development and entertainer marketing. He is also the author of "Creating Your Brand and Marketing you the Actor".

Ron has taught self-promotional marketing techniques in numerous venues. He writes an online column for the Indie Spotlight Network, focusing on the independent film industry in the southeast US.

Ron has worked on several projects for film, television, print and web series. He holds degrees in marketing and business administration.

Ron established Kaleigh Group Entertainment for the purpose of advancing actors and film makers in the independent film industry through film marketing, distribution and talent management. Since then, KGE has established itself as a leader in the area.

In 2014, Ron launched the Eastern NC Film Festival. And has recently acquired the Western NC Film Festival and is looking forward to building upon its 12 year history.

Ron is the host of the Indie Spotlight Network, a web series dedicated to spot lighting and promoting indie film makers and actors. The series features one-on-one conversations with successful, working actors and other industry professionals talking about their career journeys, turning points and lessons learned along the way. The series is designed to help empower young actors in the journeys of their own careers.

Ron is also on the Board of Directors for Eno River Media Productions, the largest nonprofit acting advocacy group in North Carolina. .

In this new book Ron builds on the concepts introduced in the first book and teaches readers how to apply those (and many new) concepts to their career to help ensure success. In the new book, Ron also teaches readers how to create and market their brands -- and, most importantly, how to create an Action Plan for career success.

Copyright © 2014, 2015 by Ron Cooper

All rights reserved. No part of this publication may be reproduced, distributed, or transmitted in any form or by any means, including photocopying, recording, or other electronic or mechanical methods, without the prior written permission of the publisher, except in the case of brief quotations embodied in critical reviews and certain other noncommercial uses permitted by copyright law. For permission requests, write to the publisher, addressed "Attention: Permissions Coordinator," at the address below.

Kaleigh Group Media

PO Box 1323

Winterville, NC 28590

EDITED by

Jana O'Keefe Henry

Samantha Armistead

**ISBN-13:
978-1515378549**

**ISBN-10:
1515378543**

Ordering Information:

Quantity sales. Special discounts are available on quantity purchases by corporations, associations, and others. For details, contact the publisher at the address above.

Orders by U.S. trade bookstores and wholesalers. Please contact Kaleigh Group Media: Tel: (252) 367-8789 or email us at media@kaleighgroupentertainment.com.

Printed in the United States of America

Disclaimer: I am not a lawyer, and by presenting to you the contents of this book and any related programs:

- Some names and identifying details have been changed to protect the privacy of individuals.

- I have tried to recreate events, locales and conversations from my memories of them. In order to maintain their anonymity in some instances I have changed the names of individuals and places, I may have changed some identifying characteristics and details such as physical properties, occupations and places of residence.

- Although the author and publisher have made every effort to ensure that the information in this book was correct at press time, the author and publisher do not assume and hereby disclaim any liability to any party for any loss, damage, or disruption caused by errors or omissions, whether such errors or omissions result from negligence, accident, or any other cause.

- The author and publisher advise readers to take full accountability for their responsibility in developing their acting career. Before practicing the skills described in this book, be advised that results may vary.

- The author has included information from his previous book "Creating Your Brand and Marketing YOU the Actor" into this book.

Table of Contents

Chapter 1   Book Introduction

Chapter 2   How Do You Want the World to Know You as an Actor

Chapter 3   Must Haves for an Actor

Chapter 4   Self Promotion Toolbox for Your Acting Career

Chapter 5   Maximizing Social Media for Your Acting Career

Chapter 6   Maximizing Your Blog for Your Acting Career

Chapter 7   Write Your Own Press Release and Article about Your Acting Career

Chapter 8   How to Network in the Acting World

Chapter 9   Building Your Entourage

Chapter 10   Buzz Building Blueprint

Chapter 11   Resources

Chapter 1
Book Introduction

Chapter 1
Book Introduction

Show business.

What a complicated lady she is. She loves you one day and ignores you the next. Yet she is always full of passion, grit and a comfortable coldness. If you are an actor at heart you yearn for her to notice you. Sometimes she does. Other times….

According to the US department of Labor (as of this writing) there are currently 640,000 paid actors in the United States. That is a lot of folks!

That means that there are a lot of people trying to lure her to notice them.

They want to get in front of her audience and express talent, heart and soul. They want the world to love them for it.

They want their talent to get them into her warm embrace.

Buuuut….

Remember you are in show *BUSINESS*. There are probably hundreds of actors who could do the role that you want. Sorry, but it's true.

YOU HAVE TO STAND OUT!

Do you think that Coca-Cola, Nike or Microsoft started one day, and became industry leaders the next?

No, of course not.

It took them many steps to get there. First they had to create their product. Then they created a marketing plan full of "secret techniques" to get that product in front of their potential customers. That plan got their customers excited enough to buy their product. The company then adjusted when necessary while staying consistent with the quality and expectation of their customers. Those customers kept buying and told their friends about it. BOOM!

That is how success was built for those businesses.

You are a business. You are selling a product. YOU, the actor. YOUR product is a culmination of your looks, experiences, skill, training and charisma.

Take a moment with that.

Yes, every single actor out there is a business.

And just like other businesses, you need to do what works. To get your customers to buy.

Okay, so how does that apply to me you ask?

Look at it like this:

1. A business creates a product. 2. That business gets people to buy that product. 3. That business wins.

Now let us compare that to your acting career.

1. You start your acting career. 2. You develop a fan base. 3. "I'd like to thank the academy for this award…"

Simple in theory, but a challenge in execution.

So…why can't you use the same marketing "secret techniques" that other businesses use every day?

You CAN!

But, you say, I am not a marketing guru. I don't know how to do all of that stuff. I don't have time to do all of that stuff.

No problem.

We will keep it quick, easy and simple. In fact, we will not even call it marketing. For some reason people are scared of that word. From now on we will call it self-promotion.

There are three main things that you need to bring to the table:

- Understand that part of your acting success is going to be based on how well you self-promote.
- Unless you have a talent manager or can hire someone....YOU have to do this.
- Have fun, change it up, but always be consistent with your quality!

We are going to cover some of the main self-promotion pillars that every actor should have.

Again, no one is expecting you to go get a college degree in marketing so that you can create a strategic marketing plan that ensures you have developed commanding market share through brand awareness by viewer conversions and differentiated integrated marketing communications.

That is just a fancy way of saying let's get all the fans we can for you!

Actors, we all want the same thing – to work! We want the chance to share our talents and become a star!

How do we get....work?

There are literally thousands of actors out there. Some will make it. Most will not. Every year more and more are added to the ranks.

It seems almost impossible to succeed.

But you want it so bad. You have always dreamed of becoming a successful actor.

Dreams lead to goals.

Goals lead to success.

But how many actors set goals?

Do you know exactly WHO YOU ARE as an actor...and why you should get work?

If not, you're not alone.

Most actors don't have a plan. They coast from job to job. Always hoping for the best.

Acting Career?

Why?

Because they don't know who they are as an actor and have no idea how to get the word out to the powers-that-be. They have no idea what they are selling. They have no idea how to self-promote. They have no specific long-term plan.

How do you even start?

Somehow you have got to come up with your brand. A brand is something that describes you in the mind of your fans.

Why is a brand important? We will get into that in a little bit, but just trust me for right now that, yes, it is important.

You have taken a big step. You have decided to do it. You are going to follow your dream. You are going to be an actor. (Just saw your name in lights, didn't you?) But right now, it seems you are stuck between your "day job" and going for every audition you can find.

Being an aspiring actor isn't easy. There are tons of other actors out there just like you.

Everyone is auditioning day after day in order to land that big break! Every year there are more aspiring actors expecting the same thing you are – to make it big!

Most will not make it. No surprise. But why?

As we have already stated, there are 59,000 doing the same thing you are, for very few roles!
How do you stick out? Why are you different than the actor sitting next to you waiting to audition?
And probably most importantly... Why should you get cast instead of anyone else?

And no, just because you want it really bad is not a good enough answer.

The film maker is trying to create their own product, their film. They want to add the best products together (you, other actors, crew, effects, storyline, etc…) so that they can sell their product.

What makes your product better than the other actors that want the role really bad?

How do you stick out? How are you remembered?

What do people think of when they think of you?

> Whatever it is they think of, that is your brand to them.
> It would probably be a good idea to make sure it is a great one!

Personal brands can be incredibly powerful and valuable when implemented and executed correctly.

So how does this relate to building an *acting* career you might be asking?

Let's try something.

What if you heard that your favorite actor/actress was about to be in a film? You have no information on the film itself, just that Will Smith, Bruce Willis, Angelina Jolie, Samuel L. Jackson (or fill in your fav here) was about to be in it. What kind of genre do you think it would be? Do you think it would be a high quality film?

The only way you could answer that question is to have some understanding of the actor.

THAT is their brand! Their looks, their delivery of their lines, the emotion they bring, etc...

The better their brand, then the better the chance for the film maker to have a successful film.

But you may be saying, "But I'm not a star yet, why do I need a Brand?"

Maybe you're not famous, YET. But, self-promotion is exactly what can help you get there!

So let's start by figuring out
what you want people to think of,
when they think of you as an actor.

1. Identify the features of your brand
Who am I?
What do I stand for?
What is it that I do/have/am that makes me different?

Answers should be less than 15 words.

List your:
- Qualities
- Personal characteristics
- Behavioral traits

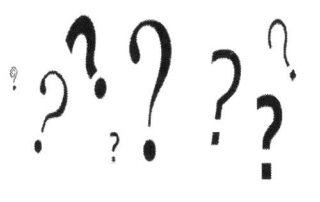

Narrow the list down to the ones that directly impact your value. Those are the features of your personal brand.

The 3 basic steps to identifying your brand:

1. **What is your "type"?**
   (Working class Jane, prep school brat, CEO, urban street youth, etc…)

2. **What describes your personality?**
   (Laid back, trustworthy, commanding, kind, generous, wild, free-spirit, etc…)

3. **What do you bring to the project?**
   (Intense brooding, air of mystery, sexiest person around, non-stop action)

Here's an exercise to get you started in identifying your own personal types & essence:

Gather a list of people (at least one family member, 5 good friends, 5 industry friends and 5 social media connections) – and ask them these following questions:

1. **What are 3 words that describe me?**
   (Playful, athletic, funny)

2. **If you didn't know me, just by looking at me and/or just hearing me voice, what would you guess I would do for a living?**
   (Teacher, lawyer, Rap star, line cook)

3. ***(Gulp) How old do I look to you?***

Thank them for the honesty and candor. Give them an autographed picture as payment (or something else as equally awesome!)

What is repeated the most? It may or may not be the personal truth about you. But most importantly it is how the public perceives you. And as you know, in the acting industry perception is reality.

This is the foundation of your Brand!

Construct it so that it is what people experience when you walk into the room!

Now, you may want to say, that this is all business talk. I am an artist. I do not want to be put into a box like that. I want to stretch my boundaries and show the world my talents.

My response is simple…. I have no problem with you being an out of the box artist, BUT you are a business. Remember you are in show BUSINESS. If you are in this business to make money then you must build your brand, get famous, and let them know ya… (After that) do anything you want to do.

Chapter 2
How Do You Want the World to Know You as an Actor

Chapter 2 — How Do You Want the World to Know You as an Actor

I personally think success is hidden from us by way of a combination lock. We must discover each correct key and then combine them in a correct order to open the lock.

In this case, the acting industry, the keys we need to discover and put into correct order are:

Key 1 – Exceeding Amount of Drive and Talent

Key 2 – Plan To Make It All Happen

Key 3 – Proper Training

Key 4 – Talent Agents / Managers

Key 5 – Media / Influencers

Key 6 – Producers / Filmmakers / Casting Directors

Key 7 – Other Actors

Key 8 – Fans

Unfortunately, the majority of actors out there will not give these eight keys the attention that each deserves; thus they will never get the big break they desire.

You now have a choice:

Do you choose to do as they do and hope for the best?

OR

Do you choose to do everything you can for the potential success of your acting career?

The following is hard work. You will have to sacrifice time, effort and energy. It will not be easy and it will be time-consuming. You will get frustrated. You will want to throw your hands up and quit.

Are you up for it?

Will you do what it takes to make YOUR acting career as successful as possible?

Seriously, think about it. Do not take the future of your career lightly. So, go ahead and think it over.

I'll wait…

…Decided to do what it takes?

GOOD! Let's get started.

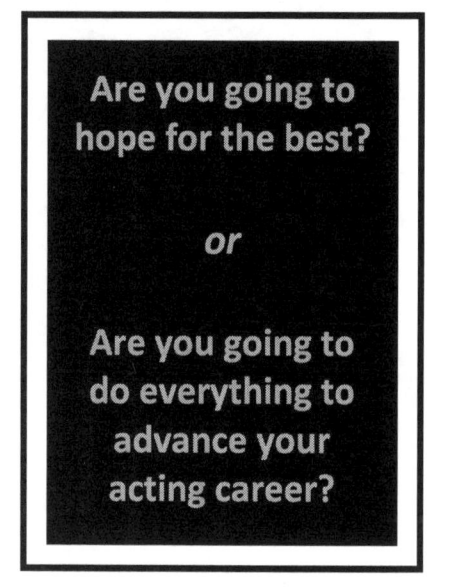

> **Are you going to hope for the best?**
>
> *or*
>
> **Are you going to do everything to advance your acting career?**

So how do you differentiate yourself from everybody else?

First impressions count. In the acting business, the first impression may be your only chance to make an impression. The first impression you make on someone is generally what will or won't lead to future work. Presenting yourself as a professional actor who is prepared and ready is the goal of that first impression.

When creating your personal brand there are a lot of tools available to you. We are going to review many of them. The trick here is to think of it as a buffet. When you eat at a buffet restaurant, you don't put everything on your plate; at least I hope you don't – that's not healthy. You pick and you choose. Maybe on a second trip you choose something else.

I want you to think of these tools the same way. Just start with a few of them. MASTER them. Then choose some more, and master them. Do this until you have got a complete and total plan.

Creating Your Brand

Branding. What do you need with branding? You are an actor. Your job is to reach deep into your soul and pull out the emotions that leave your director crying with delight for nailing it! And you do it, every time. You reach into your arsenal of technical and organic techniques and you deliver a performance that manipulates the emotions of your audience – they are putty in your hands.

Branding in some people's minds is an evasive, complicated thing that only large companies need to concern themselves with. You don't need to worry about something like that. After all, your family, friends and colleagues know you. They know your likes, dreams, goals and desires.

Branding is not important, right?

You are a person. Just like the other seven billion on this space ball. BUT…you are also an actor. An actor gets work because they get the word out that they are available to make the upcoming project awesome. How successful an actor is at getting the word out about them is a job...a business. That is why they call it show BUSINESS. That makes YOU a business. That means YOU, the person, can live your life any way you see fit. But YOU, the actor, needs to do everything you can to ensure your success. (You've got a lot of competition – how can you beat them?)

You can be the greatest actor in the world, worthy of every acting accolade and award ever made. But if you don't have an audience, it doesn't matter.

You have to be more memorable than the last guy to a casting director. If they remember you, they could potentially call you more often. More auditions mean more potential bookings. More bookings mean more fame and glory. And that, my friend, is how it works.

How do you get an audience? (When I say audience, I mean your fan base. Your fan club!)

Well, first, you need to let them know that you exist....and, of course, that you are an awesome actor. How? How do you let them know?

Easy answer:

Step 1 – Brand Yourself

Step 2 – Self-Promote Yourself

Step 3 – Work Harder Than Everyone Else

Step 4 – Success

....1,2,3,4 steps

Okay, you say to yourself. What exactly is branding, and how do I do it?

My simple definition of branding is…

What comes to someone's mind when they do not have a personal connection to a specific person, place, or thing?

Told ya…simple.

For example, you probably do not have a personal connection to Coca-Cola. By personal connection, I mean your family didn't invent Coke, or you didn't grow up running around in Coke headquarters. If you did, AWESOME!

Now, when you close your eyes and someone says, "Visualize Coca-Cola in your mind," what do you think of? Whatever you visualize – refreshing drink, logo, your name on a can, etc. – that is the "BRAND" of Coca-Cola to you.

So when a potential casting director, executive producer, or fan of yours closes their eyes and visualizes you, what will come to their mind?

That, in a nutshell, is branding…

Now, how do we make branding work for you?

Let's get started!

We have to get something straight so that we are talking about the same thing.

TYPE and BRAND

What's the difference between a type and a brand?

Your type is a combination of the five criteria found on any breakdown when a role is being cast:

- Sex
- Age Range
- Physicality (Race, short, tall, thin, heavy, light, dark, etc...)
- Job Title (surfer, barista, teen, lawyer, etc...)
- Personality Trait (sexy, extroverted, quirky, serious, etc...)

Your brand is simply combining these qualities and creating something that is uniquely YOU. Is it your smile? Your delivery of lines? Your attitude? Your intensity? You did the test earlier. You should know by now. Why will they remember you?

Without question, developing your brand and self-promotion are important to any actor's career.

Before you start planning how to tell people about YOU, the actor, you need to understand the real YOU, the actor. Your branding and marketing plans need to showcase the real YOU, the actor.

Let's build your brand first. Here's why a brand is so important.

Your brand is the foundation of all your self-promotion.

Your Brand is your ESSENCE. It is who you are. It's the thing that you don't think about, but you always bring with you. The importance of identifying your brand is that it helps you focus in on and market what makes you different from everyone else out there. This is what casting directors, agents and all other key people are looking for.

Branding yourself gives you power. People who don't know what they bring to the table can only GUESS as to why a casting director should choose them. Someone who has properly branded themselves KNOWS what they bring.

Ultimately, embracing your Brand is the key to getting your foot in the door in this business. Here are four steps to help you brand.

Step 1. How You Are Perceived.

Did you do this earlier when I asked you nicely to do so? If not, do it now! Do research. Ask other actors. Ask the crew. Ask Friends. Ask Social Media Connections.

Here's a tip to help you find out what your brand is:

1. List some adjectives that describe you.
2. Make a list of ten people (friends, family members, coworkers, cellmates, etc…).
3. Have each of them give you four adjectives that they think describe you.
4. Go through the list you receive. Are any words repeated?
5. Combine the most repeated words with something that physically describes you and create a phrase that describes you.

Step 2. Understand Your USP.

Your Unique Selling Proposition = the focus of your brand. Have you ever gone to an audition room and everyone there looked just like you?

You have two choices:

1. Feel deflated and hope for the best.

2. Be ready and prepared to use your branding to promote yourself in a calm, relaxed and confident manner.

Compare your adjectives to the most repeated list (how others see you). Was it close?

Now you can create a logline.

What's a logline?

A logline is a one sentence short phrase that sums up your unique qualities. Now you take this logline and expand it to create your brand.

Step 3. Fulfill Industry and Fan-base Expectations.

Yes, you are talented. If you are a triple threat (sing, dance and act) – YOU ROCK! But you are probably not great at everything. We all know that stage acting is different from film acting. If you are good at one, stay with that one until you become great. Does the brand that you are creating fit better for TV, film or stage? Do your best to research the role that you are auditioning.

Your Brand is your promise that you can deliver that actor. Fulfill it. Consistently.

Step 4. Make It Personal.

At some point, you will possibly have to merge the personal YOU and the acting YOU. Making it personal gives you a deeper connection to the role. This is your career, so include your values, dreams, beliefs and goals into your acting career.

Wrapping Up This Branding Thing into One Big Pile of Putty

In order to be successful, you have to understand your product before you can sell your product. You not the greatest at everything. But you can be the greatest at something. Whatever it is that makes up your USP is yours. No one else's. Own it. Appreciate what makes you special and build your brand around that.

By creating a brand, others in the industry can better understand YOU, the actor. Thus, they can better sell YOU, the actor. This means it is easier to connect to producers, directors, distributors, etc. It is not a guarantee of success, but it doesn't hurt.

Always be aware of what special qualities you bring to a role. That, my friend, becomes your brand.

Make sure that the brand *YOU, the actor,* create can be backed up by *YOU, the person*. For example, you probably shouldn't create a brand that expresses that you are a gun-toting, butt-kicking tough guy, when YOU the person just wants to snuggle with kittens.

Now, of course, you do not want to create a brand that is so concrete that it locks you down as a certain type. Make sure that what you create as a brand is flexible enough to allow you to grow as a person and as an actor.

Your brand should be reflected in your headshots, your webpage, your social media pages, and anything else that contains your likeness.

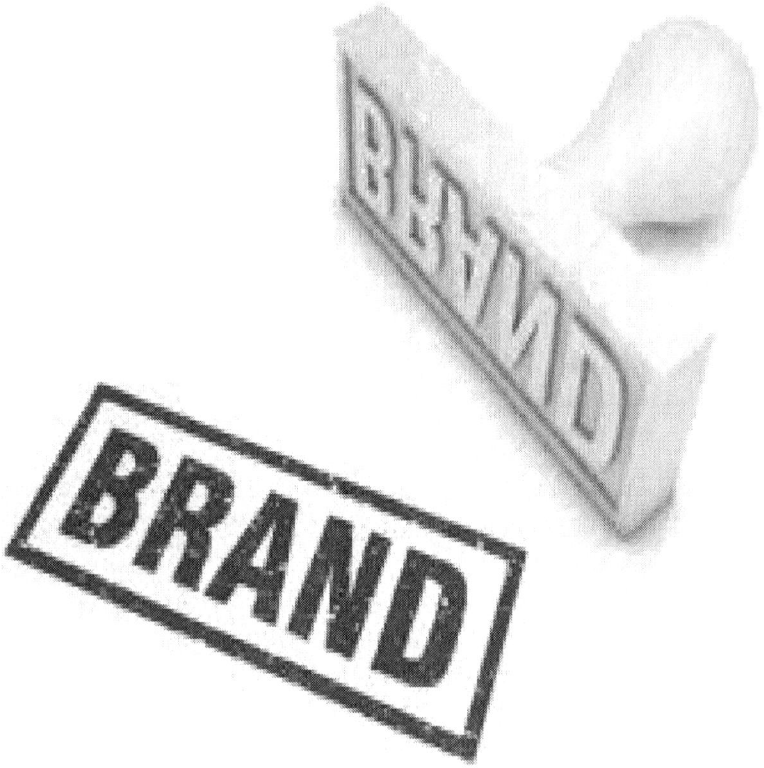
BRAND

What Is Your TYPE?

Gender: _____

Age Range:

Ask 10 random unknown people: "I am conducting a survey for my job. You will not hurt my feelings. How old do I look to you?"

(1) _____   (2) _____   (3) _____   (4) _____

(5) _____   (6) _____   (7) _____   (8) _____

(9) _____   (10) _____

Add all 10 answers together and divide by 10   (Answer) _____

Physicality

Race

Height: Short, Average, Tall

Build: Thin, Average, Heavy

Complexion: Light, Dark, Caucasian, Asian, Middle Eastern, Mediterranean, Native American, Pacific Islander

Job title

Surfer, Barista, Teen, Lawyer, etc. _____

Personality trait

Sexy, Extroverted, Quirky, Serious, etc.

_____

How Do You Differentiate Yourself From Everybody Else?

Creating Your Unique Selling Position (USP)

Meet with 10 people of influence that you do not currently know. (Community leaders, faith leaders, corporate leaders, elders, etc.)

Purpose of meeting: Before you meet with them, tell them that you want their honest first impression. Meet with them, and give them a quick bio of yourself.

Take a moment. Ask them the following:

How would you rate my appearance?

(Professional, casual, unacceptable, etc.)

How was my connection with you?

(Eye contact, body language, voice volume, lack of stuttering, etc.)

Was I concise when I spoke?

(Easy to follow, spoke with authority, etc.)

What about me sticks out to you and would make me stick out in a crowd?

(Physical characteristic, accent, way of speaking, appearance, etc.)

Now, buy them lunch, coffee or something. They just gave you important knowledge.

Creating Your Brand

Choose: TV / Film / Commercials / Theater / other

Combine the information gathered from the Type and USP worksheets to create your logline

Age Range: _____ to _____
                Low   High

Physicality: _____   _____   _____   _____
                    Race   Height   Build   Complexion

Personality trait: _____   **Job title:** _____

Logline:
_____.

EXAMPLES:
I am a 40-50 year old, average-build Caucasian, Southern Gentleman next door kind of guy.
I am a brown-eyed Yankee tough chick.
I am a gray-haired pillar of society, corporate leader, and two-timer.

The purpose of this logline is not to be type-casted. The purpose is for you to remember exactly what you are marketing. Yes, of course, go for any role that you want. However, at the core of that character is your character.

_____
_____
_____

When you go on auditions and speak with industry members
You are the representation of your product, your brand.

What is the appearance you are projecting? *(Professional, casual, unacceptable, etc.)*

How are you connecting? *(Eye contact, body language, voice volume, lack of stuttering, etc.)*

How do you come across? *(Easy to follow, spoke with authority, etc.)*

What made you stick out and be remembered in a good way? *(Physical characteristic, accent, way of speaking, appearance, conversation, offer of help, etc.)*

_____
_____
_____

Putting your brand on all the other ways you get your face out there

Your Acting Webpage / Blog	*Your Social Media Fan Pages*
Interviews	*Articles / Press Releases*
Headshots	*Handouts / Business Cards*

<u>ANY AND ALL</u> marketing tools that connect to producers, directors, distributors, fans, the media, etc. should portray your brand.

Chapter 3
Must Haves for Actors

Chapter 3 — Must Haves for an Actor

An Important Word about a Few Things.

Below are some things to keep in mind. I would suggest that you review each one and implement them at the beginning of your journey into the acting industry. These are things that are truly unique to the individual. They are, however, very important.

Elevator pitch
Once you have read this book you will have the knowledge necessary to create an awesome elevator pitch. What is an Elevator Pitch? It is a 30-60 second business description of what you do as an actor and why someone should work with you.

The reason it is called an "Elevator Pitch" because it is what you could describe about yourself to someone else during the length of an elevator ride.

You could, of course, use it on an elevator or an industry event or network party.

You only have 30-60 seconds to make a powerful first impression. You need to grab them quickly and impress the heck out of them.

Elements needed for a Powerful Elevator Pitch
- *Tell a Short Story.* A beginning, middle and end.
- *Concise.* Your time limit is 30-60 seconds.
- *Targeted.* Make specific to the listener.
- *Clear.* Simple words. Easy to follow.
- *Visual.* Use words that create a visual image in their mind.
- *Has a Hook.* Catch their attention and keep it.
- *Goal-Oriented.* What is the purpose of giving the pitch? Audition, representation, etc.?

How to create your Elevator Pitch
1. What is the end goal?
2. Write down what you do. Write it several different ways.
3. Get as many ideas as possible down on paper.
4. Write a very short story using your ideas.
5. Include spots that require interaction from your listener.
6. Leave it alone for a few days.
7. Reread and edit the story, ideas and/or interaction points.
8. Cut it to fit in 30-60 seconds.
9. Practice till you get it down.
10. Practice in front of a friend that will tell you the truth.
11. Adjust accordingly.
12. Practice in front a full length mirror to get body gestures correct.

(But you're an actor you know how to deliver! ☺)

Be positive

NEWS FLASH*** The acting industry is a harsh monster that consumes anyone with thin skin.

I know I don't need to tell you that if you want to be coddled, the acting industry is not for you.

You have got to takes steps… DAILY… to keep yourself motivated and positive. For people like me (realists) that can be a challenge. So how do you do it? How do we stay positive?

The only answer that I can give you is the natural law called 'The Law of Attraction.'

The law of attraction states: whatever you focus on most will create a frequency and attract back to your life what you are sending out. You want positive, you give positive.

Simply put... consider the way you think. Focus on thinking positively. Expect good things to happen.... to you. The theory is simple; whatever you think, you create in your life.

Some believe, some don't, but somehow in the long run, it always seems to work.

A positive attitude is important for a great many reasons. It makes our outlook better. It makes it easier for others to be around us. It makes coping with this crazy industry a little easier.

Part of our brand, our product, what we "sell" to the industry is our physical look and attitude. A positive attitude can make us a more "saleable" commodity.

Benefits of Positive Outlook:
- Inspires others
- Lowers stress levels
- Provides the opportunity for more physical and mental energy
- Provides inner strength
- Strengthens personal relationships
- Achieve your goals

How to Be More Positive:
- Make the choice to be positive
- Hang around positive people
- Practice positivity daily
- Look for the little victories
- Get inspired by quotes and stories
- Take setbacks as lessons
- Find a way to calm yourself in high stress situations

If you want to improve your life there is no better way than adopting a positive attitude.

Mentors

By a show of hands, who knows everything there is to know about the craft and industry of acting? Anyone…anyone?

Just like with anything on planet Earth, learning something is always easier when you have someone who has done it longer and been "around the block with it."

I have been around the industry for a few years and have learned a lot. I have passed that knowledge along to those behind me in this journey we call the acting industry. They have always been appreciative. I don't say that as a boast, I say it to say this. There are other people in the industry that I get around and I feel dumbfounded and don't know anything. I do all I can to soak up their knowledge and I am very appreciative of it. It just goes to show you, that there is always someone smarter.

I always try to live by the saying, "If I am the smartest person in the room, then I need to find a new room."

If you haven't considered an acting mentor before, you might wish to reconsider.

Why should you have a mentor?
As I have already mentioned, there is no need to reinvent the wheel. If someone can show you an easier way, then why not capitalize on their knowledge?

What is a mentor?
A mentor is someone you respect and who has knowledge that you need. Additionally, they are in a position to advise you. So you can think of them as a mentor, coach or advisor. They can assist with day to day situations or just be there when you get "stuck."

Who makes a good mentor?
It MUST be someone you respect. Put simply, you believe they have already gone down the path that you have chosen. You believe that they possess knowledge that you want. I suggest someone who can be brutally honest with you. Not for the purpose of hurting you, but to provide honest insight with the sole motivation for helping you grow.

How do I get a Mentor?
Create a list from people you have or would like to work with on a project. If you know them personally, tell them. If you do not know them, ask someone who does for an invitation. If that doesn't work, make a list of your top ten movies. Who worked on those films? You can always contact them through email or social media.

Fashion Sense
Let me be the first to say, I am not a fashionista. I am most comfortable in jeans and a t-shirt. So I had to do a lot of research for this section.

I didn't need any research, however, to tell me this one simple rule in our industry. Your physical appearance is completely and totally judged. It is a necessity. People WATCH films. Therefore, they watch what we look like. So, we must look right for the project.

Plus, it makes sense. When we audition, we want the role. When we step on a Red Carpet, we want to look good. We have already agreed that we are a product. I ask you, would you go to a store and buy a product that was not presented in the best way possible? Of course not. Why should we offer any less for ourselves?

It is no secret that a well-dressed person is much appreciated in society. Many actors are admired for their dress sense. A pleasing personality is essential, and clothes also enhance ones' appearance. This goes along, of course, with proper grooming.

How to create a fashion sense?
Many people watch their favorite actor and dress similarly.
Fashion magazines provide good information on how to dress.
Find someone with a fashion sense you respect (there is that Mentor thing again).
Quality clothing stores are a great choice as well.
Fashion websites and blogs are good.

> **TIP*** Please do not go broke trying to reload your closet with the latest fashions. Get 3-5 outfits that are interchangeable and you will be good to go!**

Clothes make a lot of difference as to how you look. Even an ordinary looking person can come across attractive if his or her choice of clothes is appropriate. The opposite is also true. Bad clothes, bad look.

Keep in mind: What you look like (fashion, grooming and body language) is the only thing that other people can see about us. I mean, have you ever heard anyone say, "Check out the personality on that guy!"

This should go without saying, but I am going to say it anyway.

Stay in shape. Stand up straight. Have good posture. Fashion is not just about what you wear, it's also about how you wear it. Taking better care of your body can be as simple proper diet and exercise. Just shoot for a little healthier lifestyle than you had yesterday. This allows you to feel better, be more confident and look better. I used to own a gym, so yes, I know this works.

Most importantly - Be yourself!
The most important aspect of developing your own style is remaining true to yourself.

Mantra

So now we can take what we have learned in the last few pages of this section and mix it together into 2-3 sentences that describe our outlook on this whole process and apply it to the rest of this book and into our acting career!

An example might be:

I am going to keep my attitude in check so that I portray a positive and motivating attitude for myself and those around me. If I need help I will develop relationships with potential mentors to help me obtain success in my acting career, and I will look good while I am doing it!

Actor's Access / 800 Castings / IMDb

There are several websites that the "big boys" look at on a constant basis. Yes, on the West Coast there are many more. But we are going to focus more on these.

These are three of them.

Yes, there are others, but we are going to let these represent all of them.

These sites have free and paid sections.

I will suggest to you to maintain the paid versions. It offers more options for the sites, but more importantly, provides a perception that you are professional enough to invest in the tools to make you better at your craft.

You must keep these up to date!

Before you can have a massive load of fans, you have to be known to the Producers, Film Makers and Casting Directors.

You need to go where there are.

Actors Access
www.actorsaccess.com

800casting
www.800casting.com

IMDb
www.imdb.com

Chapter 4
Self-Promotion Toolbox for Your Acting Career

Chapter 4   Self-Promotion Toolbox for Your Acting Career

I think I can be confident in saying that the Internet is probably here to stay.

Most people use the Internet often. They use it for personal, recreation, academic and business reasons.

They play games, look up reviews, shop, set up appointments, communicate, and so much more.

My point here is simple. A lot of people spend a lot of time on the Internet.

Okay, and....?

Well, let's play this out. If a lot of people are constantly on the Internet...probably a good-size amount of those people like films and actors. Of those people that like films and actors.... Why can't a percentage of them like YOU, the actor?

Here is how we are going to do it.

There are many types of marketing delivery. We are going to focus on just three of them. They are:

Push Marketing

A direct approach by a company to get you to buy their product or service.
Definition Example: Coca-Cola puts a commercial on TV. You like what you see. You go buy the product.

What we are going to use:
- Actor's Access
- 800 Castings
- IMDb
- Press Kit
- Directories
- Talent Agents
- Talent Managers
- Business Cards
- Handouts
- Meet & Greets
- Premieres / Wrap / Release Parties
- Public Service Announcements
- Speaking Engagements
- Charity Events

Pull Marketing

A company markets to the end user (the person who will actually use the product or service).
Definition Example: Pharmaceutical companies put an advertisement on TV for you to "ASK YOUR DOCTOR ABOUT…" You (the end user) can't get the drug without the prescription.

What we are going to use:
- Your Website
- Marketing / PR
- On Set
- Meet & Greets
- Premieres / Wrap / Release Parties
- Speaking Engagements
- Charity Events
- Merchandise

Content Marketing
This type of marketing came along with the Internet. The company befriends it customers on its website, social media sites and other Internet sites. The company may offer additional information about the product, games, surveys and chat sessions. Its purpose is to provide the customer with a more involved feeling. You are not being told to buy something; it is supposed to feel more like two friends conversing with each other.

What we are going to use:
- Your Website
- Your Social Media Pages
- Your Blog
- Press Releases About You
- Articles About You
- Social Media Endorsers
- On Set
- Meet & Greets
- Red Carpets
- Premieres / Wrap / Release Parties
- Public Service Announcements
- Speaking Engagements
- Charity Events
- Interviews
- Merchandise

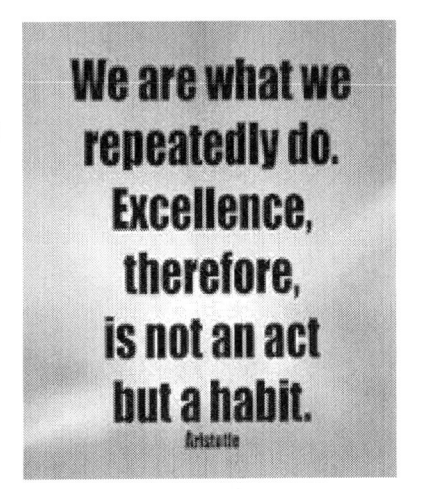

> We are what we repeatedly do. Excellence, therefore, is not an act but a habit.
> Aristotle

Don't worry; we're going to break each of these down for you. We are going to create your marketing plan utilizing these marketing deliveries.

…Yes, each one of them.

…Yes, we are keeping it simple.

…Yes, it will be easy.

…Don't give me that look.

Right now, all you need to know is the difference between each of them.

No, there is not going to be a test.

We will dig a little deeper and discuss how each of these are used as we move along.

You will probably notice – because you are awesome – that some of these are in more than one delivery system. That is because they are used in different ways in different systems.

We are not going to put these in any kind of order because they are all very useful tools. The important thing is to build one, get it right, and then build the next one. Self-promotion only works if you have something to promote and you have the resources to promote.

Press Kits

IF you are planning on being a successful actor, IF you truly want to get famous, then you MUST have a press kit. If you do not get anything else out of this book, let it be this: ALWAYS have a fantastic press kit.

One of the biggest mistakes an actor can make is not having a press kit.

Why do I need a press kit?

- You can use it to get in front of Agents, Managers and Casting Directors.
- It showcases your achievements.
- It is what media people need to put you in their media.

What is a press kit?

Images: One of the most important things for your press kit is pictures. After all, a picture tells a thousand words, right? Your headshot, picture of you on a red carpet, backstage at an interview or a production shot. Just be sure to not to overdo it with too many pictures.

Biography: This is a brief summary of your acting career and your life. It needs to include big and shiny moments as well as dark times (that you are comfortable making public).

Articles: Collect everything. Blog posts, articles and press releases. Include articles specifically about you or about projects that you have been involved with. Just make sure you had a significant role in the project.

Current Projects: In what project are you currently involved? Include everything that you have permission to include. What is important to show here is that you are an in-demand actor. This also keeps it up-to-date and relevant.

Website: As an actor, you are a business. Every successful business has a website. You need people to find you and contact you. Make sure your contact information is easy to find.

Social Media: The social media section is meant to display the brand that you have created for yourself as an actor. Use social media to advance your brand, your sponsors and your career.

Charity Work: Charity work showcases your ability to be able to perform but also give back to the community. It potentially can open up the door for you to be an "Ambassador" of an organization that is important to you.

Endorsements/Sponsorships: If a company out there endorses you, put it here. Even if it is just a friend's company, this shows that you're marketable.

Business Cards

Part of your self-promotion plan includes networking. It involves getting face-to-face with others in the industry. It involves impressing them enough so that they will see your awesomeness and want to share it in their next project. They need to leave that event with something in their hands about you. Remember, you are a business. Businesses use business cards.

Your business card MUST look professional. It must be well-designed. It must visualize your brand. It must impress the person receiving it. It must show that you are committed to your craft and serious about the success of your career. Tall order to fill, but that is the nature of the beast. Plus, if you could provide a visual representation of your awesomeness, that is a heck of a lot better than saying, "hit me up on Facebook."

The only recommendation I have for the actual look of your business card is that it MUST have a picture of you on it. After all, YOU are the brand!

Get business cards made. Keep them on you. When someone asks what you do, give your elevator speech and hand them a card. You are a professional: be prepared. When you go to networking events, have a plan to give out "X" amount of cards to key people.

IMPORTANT NOTE: Do not act like a used car salesman. When you speak with the key people, stay in control. They will learn how awesome you are. You don't have to show them all of your awesomeness in thirty seconds. Be smooth.

Things you should be doing when it comes to designing and handing out your business card:

Keep it simple. Avoid a flashy design. You do not want them impressed with the card. You want them impressed with the person on the card.

You should have your main headshot picture on your business card.

Remember that your card will not turn into a cherished keepsake to the people you give it. You may see it in the trash can. (Yes, this has happened to me.) It is not personal. It is just part of business.

Please, please, please make sure your contact information is easy to read.

Don't waste your money by handing them out to everyone. Just give it to the people that will benefit your career.

Business cards are not going to get you work! They connect you to people who can. So don't think handing out a card equates to you getting a role.

Handouts / Postcards

A handout is a step up from a business card for those in the acting industry. A handout is usually around four by six inches. On the front are your name, full body, the quarter body shot, and a headshot. On the back is a quick resume of the acting work that you have done. The handout is your follow-up to your business card. Give your business card to everyone. But after you have been smooth and carried on the conversation and the person has shown interest, then and only then, give them your handout.

Here are some of the advantages of postcards:

You can communicate a short message without being overwhelming.

You can have several different genres made up depending on who you are giving them.

If you mail them, the recipient will see it without having to open it, like they would a headshot/resume.

Very few people are annoyed by receiving a postcard.

General postcards with no message don't work. It's just not compelling enough. You are a professional…sell your product, which is YOU, the actor.

Use them along with a press release to casting agents and filmmakers about happenings in your career.

Send them to fans about upcoming roles.

Send them to agents and managers that you want to sign.

It is much more a hands-on approach than social media.

Use them as invitations to upcoming events.

Do not use preprinted labels. Hand-write every address if you mail them. It looks more personable. Plus, people usually open a hand written envelope.
Continually update your mailing list BEFORE you mail anything. Design it to fit the genre.

Use a P.O. Box, your agent's, or manager's address. Never use your personal addresses.

If you are going to use someone else's likeness or logo, make sure that you have permission.

Make sure the handout/postcard is a standard mailing size. If you want to print in small quantities, use one of the large drug store photo programs.

Again, postcards will not get you the job. But they can get you in touch with the person that can.

Send postcards out about every 2 months. Clean and simple is always your best option. DO NOT send out a handout/postcard on an upcoming project for which you do not have the clearance yet. Don't break any confidentiality agreements.

Keep it professional. Don't be a critic of your own work. Just give 'em the facts and fun.

Remember the purpose of sending out these postcards is part of your marketing strategy. Do not exaggerate; only tell what you can prove.

ALWAYS, ALWAYS, ALWAYS make yourself look good!

PROMOTE YOURSELF

Actor Reel

Would you buy a car without test driving it first? Probably not.

A film maker wants to kick the tires before hiring you. The easiest way they can do this is to view your talent reel.

You say you don't have one. You say you haven't gotten around to putting one together.

YOU are your most important product! YOU are what you are selling.

Video yourself performing monologues.

Act out a scene with other actors.

You can do it from a good mobile device on a tripod (not hand held).

You can do this until you have a higher quality reel.

Some of the film makers that I know will pass right over you if they do not know you and you don't have a reel. Please, please, please…create a talent reel!

Primary mission:

ALWAYS look like your brand in the public eye. PERIOD!

You work hard at perfecting your craft. You memorize. Get your body to tell the story of the script. Perfect it with your blocking.

So make sure your actor reel shows that.

We all know that your actor reel is video montage of your best work in two minutes.

But, Ron, I am just starting acting. I don't have anything to montage myself into a reel, you say. I respond, "No problem!" Start off by filming yourself reciting your best monologue. Have someone interview you. Get with some actor friends and create a short film (for the sole purpose of filming you). As you get more work, substitute until you have the best reel in the industry.

Remember, your actor reel is a video display of you performing your craft. This is what you will put on your website, industry sites and your social media pages. This is the first impression that others will see that do not know how awesome you are...yet.

Now let us talk a little bit of how to put this thing together.

Keep this in mind. This may be the first thing someone sees in regards to your work. You want to make the right impression. Your acting is great – no problem there.

BUT...

What if is a poor filming, horrible angles, bad lighting, terrible sound, or anything else that could make you look bad?

Chances are that is what they remember.

So let's break it down and see what we come up with. (I hate ending a sentence with a prepositional phrase, but I digress.) And remember, just because you are in a scene does not mean that it has to be in your actor reel. Only choose the best of the best of you!

Filming

If you are cutting a scene from a project you are in, then great. Hopefully, everything looks and sounds fine. Whoever you get to create your actor reel, make sure the tweak the sound, contrast, and all of the other fun things to make you like the star that you are.

If you are creating your own, make sure the person filming is using a quality product. Remember, the final product is going to make your first impression; so make sure it is of high quality.

Lighting

Choose (or make) a scene that provides you in a good light. Appropriate lighting obviously depends on the genre of the film. For example, a horror film will not have the same lighting scheme as a love story. But what is important that you are clearly seen in the shot.

Sound

The quickest turnoff of any film is the sound. Too high, too low, or muffled, and it can kill the mood of a film faster than a parent at a teenage rave. If you have an otherwise good scene, is there any way to tweak and make it sound better? If not, don't use it.

Overall Appeal

Again, YOU, the actor, are a business. Your business puts out products. One of your products is your actor reel. You get paid by this product in the way that people respond to it. If they respond positively, you get fans and the opportunity to do bigger and better things. If they respond negatively to it, you don't. Not trying to be harsh, just trying to be real with you. (I want you to succeed!)

Hand Out Your Face Attitude
Maybe it sounds weird to you that we are including an attitude in the middle of your toolbox.

BUT, this attitude must be a part of what you are trying to accomplish. It is just as important as your headshot, resume or any other self-promotion tool.

Here is why.

You can have put together the greatest press kit, hired the greatest photographer for your head shot, and have a killer resume.

However, if you do not have the gumption to get it out there, no one will ever know you. Some people may look at this as being pushy, cocky or some other negative connotation. NO, it is not. You are a business. Every successful business has someone who sells their product. Right now, that salesperson is you. As you get more of a career and your awesomeness flows, then your agent, manager and PR firm will do the selling of you… but, right now it is you. This is your career. This is your brand. This is your business. This is YOU!

You may have already developed a great team. They work hard to make you successful. But they are not you.

YOU have to go out there and make this work.
YOU have got to lead your team to help you be more successful.
YOU have got to be the driving force behind your success.

Most importantly…
YOU have got to believe in yourself.
YOU have got to know YOU are worth the recognition.
YOU have got to know that you are good enough.
YOU have got to know that you are worthy.
YOU have got to stay focused.
YOU must persevere!

Your agent, your web guy, your photographer, and all of the others will always work hard for you. You are the one with the vision. You are the one that created the brand. They have faith enough to join your team, because they believe in what you are doing. Make sure you do, too.

Headshots
Why is your headshot on of the most important tools for being a working actor?

Most casting directors really focus on the headshot. They will look at your eyes to see if they can see what they are looking. The style of the headshot usually is not a deciding factor. When they have your headshot (with your resume on the backside of it) they will put it in the either the *KEEP* or *MAYBE NEXT TIME* pile. Then they review them and give their final selections to the film maker, producer, etc...

The purpose of this book is not to tell you who should take your headshot or how it should be done. Our purpose here is to use the headshot as a self-promotion tool.

Your picture is not called a three-quarter shot; it's called a headshot that means a shot of your head. It should never focus on a "cool" background. Usually a simple clear photo with a neutral background is all that you need.

If you are paying for the shoot, then you're the boss—not the photographer. The photographer can make suggestions, but you are the end product. You know how you want you to look.

What should the basis of a headshot include?

It should be a shoulders shot. Your shoulders should be squared off to camera, not turned away. The camera should be level with your eyes. Don't have your hands on your face. Try to get the reflection of the lights in your eyes. It should be simple and straightforward. Your expressions should be subtle. NEVER EVER touchup your headshot.

If you have a manager, it is one of the primary jobs that they should do for you. But we are going to discuss it here, just so that we are thorough.

Have several headshots made up. Let them portray your look in different ways. Obviously, if you do anything to alter your look…get new shots.
Keep a few close by at all times. You never know. ☺

Resume

Keep in mind, the purpose of this book is not to teach you how to prepare your acting resume (however, that is very important and should be done correctly). The purpose of this book is to help you prepare the best self-promotion tools for you.

Your acting resume is going to be seen by casting directors, film makers, producers, etc…

What do they want to see on your resume?

- Your successes
- Production companies you have worked with
- Characters you've played
- Directors and producers you've worked with
- Teachers you've had
- Special skills
- Credits that stand out

(A guest star role on a network show carries more weight than one on an unknown web series)

Keep your resume crisp and clean so that our eyes go straight to the most important details.

Put your credits by and large in chronological order

If you do not yet have any impressive credits, focus on training that you have had.

KEEP IT UP TO DATE. KEEP IT UP TO DATE. KEEP IT UP TO DATE.

Do I need to repeat it again?

Do not get in the habit of doing work and saying, "I will update it later."

You are a professional. Act like it.

What if you have been working a lot and have done five or six jobs since the last time you updated it, then (as always happens in this industry) there is a call tomorrow for the best role of your life – all you have to do is submit your headshot and résumé. Please, be the professional that you are and be prepared.

Chapter 5
Maximizing Social Media for Your Acting Career

Chapter 5 Maximizing Social Media for You're Acting Career

You're Website

A website for YOU, the actor, is not only important – it is necessary. It is like having a publicist that never sleeps. It provides the opportunity for everyone to see your headshots, actor reel, articles, contact forms and anything else you want to put in front of your audience.

Make sure that all of the great things that are happening in your acting career, all of the press releases, stories about you at meet and greets and your help with charities are easily accessible on your website where they can be read by your fans.

A well-built website can be the best self-promotional tool you can have as an actor. A strong website is the first step to achieving success online. Your website MUST represent you.

What is the benefit of having a strong website if people can't find it? You must ensure that you have proper search engine optimization (SEO) and are listed in appropriate online directories.

Part of having a great website is to convert folks that casually come to your website and turn them into fans. Make sure that you have an OPT IN feature so that you can gather their contact information to let them know of events coming up, new merchandise or projects being released.

Most important rule when building a website for YOU, the actor...Keep it simple! Keep it easy to navigate, keep it clean and of course, make sure it has professional look.

You have several options:
- Do It Yourself
- Get A Web Designer
- Let A Talent Marketing Firm Create It And Run It For You

Whichever option you choose, you need to decide exactly what your site needs and what you need to avoid.
Here are some mistakes you need to avoid:

Amateur Design – DON'T LET IT LOOK CRAPPY!!! For the people that do not know you, this is their first impression. Make sure it reflects professionalism. Make it easy to navigate.

A Static Website – Your website should not be a poster. You can't change a poster. You can't update a poster. Once you have looked at a poster, you do not need to look at again, because it is not going to change. Keep it up to date. Change it often. Make your audience want to keep coming back to it.

Do Not Use Flash – It is quickly becoming outdated. It does not do well with mobile devices. Use your creativity in other ways.

Do Not Post In Third-Person Updates – I am going to assume here that you are not a big star....yet. So, don't act like you have a publicist writing everything...People can tell. Plus, remember the content marketing we spoke about earlier...give it the personal touch. Even when you make it big, keep it personal.

Do Not Come Across As A Used Car Salesperson – Don't you hate it when ads come across overly excited and basically screaming how much you need their product? Chances are, if you hated that...so does your audience. Be real, be honest, have fun.

Do not post any intimate photos. They can come back to hurt your career. Don't share anything nude or sexually explicit.

Never, ever post any photos or info about your children, personal residence or address. Don't make it easy for a stalker to follow or harass you. Do not talk about or show photos of your spouse, unless they are directly related to the work in the photo.

Okay, so enough about mistakes. Here's what you absolutely NEED!

1. Welcome Page. Use a headshot that most honestly portrays the "real you." Even though this picture is the real you, it needs to be a professional picture. Remember, this is the first thing they see. Include your favorite inspiring quote. This is a point to connect to you, so do it. Use welcoming colors. Don't use tables!

2. Blog. This is where you get to say what you want to your fans, potential agents and potential directors. ALWAYS keep it positive. Do not discuss politics, religion or hardcore topics, unless this fits within the brand that you have created. Write in a personal format – the purpose is to develop a connection to the reader. The more your reader connects to you, the more they will like you, trust you and hopefully hire you.

3. Headshots. Have several different looks. Different looks (smiling, serious, brooding, etc.), different outfits (biker, corporate, Western, etc.), different locations (indoors, outdoors, interesting background, etc.), different genres (commercial, movie poster, romantic book cover, etc.). Show as many looks as you can while being consistent with your type and brand. This can help a casting director visualize you for an upcoming role.

4. Resume. Number one rule….KEEP IT UP TO DATE!

5. Bio. Keep this to four short paragraphs. Formally introduce yourself. Highlight your career. Include testimonials from actors and directors that you have worked with. Include your training, credits and recent roles.

6. Actor Reel. Upload your reel to YouTube or Vimeo and provide a link to easily get to it. You can choose to maintain your privacy by making your video unlisted on YouTube. This means only the people that go to your website and click on the link can view it. Make your career experience look like a hot trailer from a hit movie, and it will sell you!

7. Social Media Links. Make sure you include links to all of your social media pages. Twitter, Facebook Fan Page, LinkedIn, Stage 32, Instagram, etc. Encourage people to sign up for them.

8. Photo Gallery. This includes promotional shots, behind-the-scenes photos, press photos and exciting action photos. This shows you as a real actor. Also, use these pictures on your social media pages. For every event you attend (readings, workshops, red carpet events, industry related party, etc.) be prepared to take pictures so that you can create a visual history of your career. Additionally, when you travel, play sports, work with charities, etc. always get photos of those things that you can post. The purpose is to enhance your marketability as an actor.

9. A Business Email. Most websites have the option of creating emails through them. Create one that is professional. The ONLY thing you use it for is to build your career. Contacting your agent, responding to interview requests or anything else that will advance your career. Use your personal email for personal things.

A website is one of the most important promotional tools for an actor. The easier you can make it for someone to get to know you, the better chance you have of making an impact with them.

Your Social Media Pages

One of the best ways to gain some traction in obtaining fans is without a doubt...social media.

Obviously, one of the biggest goals in having a social media strategy is gaining followers:

Gaining Followers
When your followers try to engage with you, respond! Remember, this is why you are doing this in the first place. Very rarely are you going to keep fans if you ignore them; plus, it is just rude. You will gain new followers quicker if people see that you take the time to write back. But do keep in mind that when you post, only a percentage of your followers will see your post.

DO NOT use your social media to oversell yourself and shove yourself down your followers' throats. Use it to build a rapport. Your social media platform is not a broadcast channel. It's a place that people get together to share and have conversations.

Building Your Social Media Strategy

Do not use your personal pages as your acting pages. Take a very methodical approach. Create fan pages for the sole purpose of promoting your acting career. EVERYTHING that happens on those pages is, in some way, to advance your acting career. Pictures, videos, statements or anything else...it is all related to building your career.

In the early stages as you are building your acting career and developing your brand, you must control all of the content, engagements and relationships being built across your social media channels.

The social media site will dictate how often you need to post on that particular social media fan page. A general rule of thumb should be five to fifteen times per week. Key times to post are between 11am to 10pm. A word of warning – one of the main reasons people stop following a brand is because they post too frequently…. So just be careful.

Each social media site uses its own rules. Make sure you use the right language and tags so that people can discover you.

People are selective about connecting with others that they don't yet know. Make sure that they are happy to follow your actor fan pages. Obviously, a goal should be to get your followers to connect with you on as many of your social media pages as possible.

Make sure that all of your profiles stay up to date.

Just remember that social media is part of your bigger marketing campaign. Please do not get into a habit of posting once a day and thinking you have done enough. Until you are a household name...you've got to put work into it to make it happen.

Over the past few years we have seen the rapid rise of social media. Ignoring it to advance your career can be a big mistake. Social media has changed how we communicate and is probably here to stay for quite a while. While it is a great tool, it must also be used with care. It is constantly evolving, so be ready to change with it. Any social media strategy works best when it is targeted to a specific audience. Not only is social media useful for marketing, but it is also a great way to gauge feedback from your fans, fellow actors, film makers or anyone else in the industry. Remember, you must work on your brand identity when using social media. Social media gives you wonderful opportunities to reach your audience. Spend time on your social media strategy.

There are many ways to market you to film makers, agents, casting directors and your fans. Without a doubt, the easiest is social media. Social Media has become a necessary marketing strategy. Social Media affords you the opportunity to touch your industry and fan base fairly easily on a daily basis.

Social Media is going to be one of the key marketing strategies that you need to use for your marketing. Be consistent with your efforts and you'll generate the momentum you're looking for to grow your industry and fan base.

Facebook

These tips will help you have better success on Facebook.
- Publish 3 updates daily
- Syndicate your blog posts regularly (with links back to your website)
- Monitor for comments; reply as needed

Twitter

On twitter, you need to know this.
- Publish 5-6 tweets daily, including your blog posts
- Retweet 3-5 relevant tweets daily
- Retweet influencers
- Respond to tweets
- Follow 15 relevant users or brands daily
- Follow new people everyday
- Use #hashtags to follow or lead conversations
- Track mentions and keywords

Linkedin

LinkedIn should be used for the business side of show business
- Publish 5-6 updates daily
- Participate in industry groups 2-3 times weekly
- Like or comment on 3 pieces of content daily
- Scan industry groups a few times a week
- Connect with 5 new people weekly

Google+

Make sure you use these tips
- Promote posts from influencers in the industry
- Publish 3 updates daily, including your blog posts
- Use Circles to create relevant connections
- Add 10-15 people to circles weekly
- Make sure your posts are public

YouTube

YouTube is the second largest search engine... use it to your advantage
- Create a video of your monologues
- Ensure that your Talent Reel is visible
- Post a new video weekly
- Ask questions from fans and create videos to address them
- Add fun in your videos
- Use a videographer for events that you attend

Directories

It doesn't hurt to put your headshot on multiple website directories. I have listed a few here, but they are constantly changing. To look for more acting directories a simple perusal through your favorite search engine will provide a long list. The reason you want to do this is important, because it provides an additional listing when people search your name.

You must, of course, tag the picture properly. If it is listed in a directory, you will be limited as to what you can do. If possible, provide a link so that when someone clicks on the picture it sends them to your website.

Below is a list (at the time of this writing) of online actor directories. This is by no means a complete list. It is intended to give the reader (you) an idea of where to look.

Actors & Extras | Talent Directory - StarNow
www.starnow.com/Talent-Directory/United-States/Actors/

Actor Hub - Free Online Actor and Casting Call Directory
www.actorhub.com/

Spotlight - Professional acting jobs, auditions and castings.
www.spotlight.com/

Players Directory - Actor Information
https://www.playersdirectory.com/info/actors.php

Actors and Actresses: Directories - Dmoz
http://www.dmoz.org/Arts/Performing_Arts/Acting/Actors_and_Actresses/

UK Talent Directory | Actors, Models, Singers and More.
www.castingnow.co.uk/talent-directory

Backstage Resources | Call Sheet Database for Agents.
www.backstage.com/resources/

California's Film Industry Production Services Directory
www.film.ca.gov/ProductionTools_Production

CastNet | The UK Casting Agents resource for Casting.
https://www.castnet.co.uk/

Extras
www.extras.com/

Disclaimer: *Placement of these directories is solely from research and is for informational purposes only. I have no connection with any of these and cannot be held responsible for any outcome of their use. Websites come and go. As always, user beware.*

Chapter 6
Maximizing Your Blog for Your Acting Career

Chapter 6   Maximizing Your Blog for Your Acting Career

Starting a blog is a great option to help you connect with other people and to build your brand. Blogging is an excellent way to share your experiences as an actor as well as provide a personal connection to others.

The experiences and challenges that you have in your acting career will probably differ from other actors around you. The lessons that you learn throughout your career can prove to be valuable to your fans, fellow actors, film makers and others in the entertainment industry. You can write (or video) about a day in the life, audition experiences, a meet-and-greet experience or anything else you would like to discuss.

Just make sure that people want to follow your stories. Use it to share stories and create networking opportunities.

Once you do start blogging, you must plan to post to your blog often. Every day is different, exciting and challenging. Your readers will start to gain an understanding of who you are as you build your brand through this marketing pillar.

You can create a blog through one of many free blog sites. Blogger is probably one of the easiest to use and best recognized. Not to mention that it is owned by Google, so that will definitely help with finding you in a web search.

Having a blog is one of the easiest and efficient ways to develop your fan base.

- Write 2-3 blog posts each week
- Share each post more than once on Facebook, Twitter, Google+, LinkedIn
- Subscribe to 2 new blog feeds weekly
- Share 3 blog posts from your feeds daily
- Distinguish "YOU". Personalize your content. Make it different from other actors.
- How much of your character have you put into it?
- Create a way to track your followers and keep them engaged… There are a lot of distractions out there
- Create a content schedule. This is a list of things to discuss and the days that you will write about them

Blogging Ideas

- Tell stories about solutions to problems that have worked for you.
- Upcoming events
- Upcoming projects (with proper permissions)
- Projects you recently finished
- Your upbringing
- How you got started
- Questions from fans
- Keep paragraphs short. Bullet points where you can. Readers want visual breaks.
- Read it a few times before you post it to make sure grammar and spelling are correct
- Add pictures whenever you can
- Encourage fans to leave comments

Connect your posts with Google Authorship and other blog directories.

Make sure your website, social media pages and blog are connected.

Make sure fans can easily subscribe to your blog.

Your blog's success depends on you giving your target audience content they will crave and share.

Take a look at the leaders in the industry. What are they doing that looks successful? Can you easily incorporate any of it?

Chapter 7

Writing Your Own Press Releases and Articles about Your Acting

Chapter 7 — Write Your Own Press Release and Articles About Your Acting Career

A press release is a written communication directed at members of the news media for the purpose of announcing something that you believe to be newsworthy.

I personally believe that if press releases are used properly, they can be a very powerful self-promotional tool. That being said, we are going to spend some time on this subject.

Websites have changed the way that you would traditionally submit a press release. There used to be two ways to get a press release to a news agency – either by email or fax. Now there are many online sources that allow you to submit a press release (some are free and some are fee-based), but you have a lot more choices.

Why is this important?

Because when you submit a press release the news agency is not obligated to run it. It is their choice. By submitting to multiple news agencies you have a better opportunity to have your press release run.

The purpose of a press release is simple: to attract favorable media attention to yourself. Press releases can announce anyone of many newsworthy events, such as introduction, upcoming projects, news conference, current releases, etc.

If you're wondering what exactly should be covered in a press release, think along the lines of a very straight to the point newspaper article. The more newsworthy you make your career, the more coverage you can get.

A press release is short and is designed to pique interest. The press release should contain all of the "who," "what," "where," "when," "how," and most importantly "why" questions.

There is definitely a knack to writing a press release, even though the ultimate goals are usually awareness and promotion. Editors don't like promotion, though, so crafting a press release to appeal to an editor is key. There's no guarantee that any press release will ever be published, but by taking a professional approach with the reputable editors of respected publications, the probability is good that you'll get some coverage. Just keep plugging away.

Parts of a Press Release

First, a press release begins with contact information (name, phone number and email address of the person who wrote the release) up at the top left hand corner of the page, as if you were addressing a letter.

Skip a line.

Sometimes you need to have your story released immediately. If so type: FOR IMMEDIATE RELEASE/To Be Released on XX/XX/XX

Other times you might have a little time. If so provide the date it needs to be released.

Skip a line.

Next is the headline. The title should be four or five words that quickly describe the press release and hook the reader to continue reading. Avoid using standard or cliched titles. Type the title in BOLD print and center it on the page.

Skip a line.

Realign your margin to the left. Next put the location of where your news is taking place, followed by a dash (-), the date and another dash. For example:

"Raleigh, NC – 19 July 2015 –"

Skip a line.

WHO, WHAT, WHERE, WHEN, WHY and HOW.
This first paragraph should explain why this news is important and why someone should read farther.

Skip a line.

The second paragraph should be shorter. It should just give the journalist your contact information.

Skip a line.

The third paragraph includes the secondary details and should expand on the first paragraph.

Then 3 number signs ### centered at the bottom of the page

Helpful Tips and Reminders

- Outline it before you write
- Keep it simple
- Be brief, positive and specific
- Be accurate
- Don't repeat yourself!
- Proof-read and spell check
- Proof-read and spell check again
- Have it to them at the START of the business day
- Send it to multiple sites
- Don't be surprised if they do not run it

Every media site on the internet is in constant need of content. Yes, even in this age of social media. As an actor, you can utilize press releases to help create your own buzz! It doesn't matter if you are trying to obtain interviews and media attention, or you just want to inform industry contacts of what is going on with your acting career, press releases are a great addition to your marketing arsenal.

Follow up.

Setup a Google Alert and collect any media as a result of your press release. Forward what you receive to your social media sites, blog and website.

Here are several factors that can make a story newsworthy. Timeliness is the most important.

Scandal: This kinda goes without saying. How can you twist a bit of scandal into your story?

Local: Most news organizations cover a specific geographic range. Make sure the story is within their area of coverage.

Underdog: People want to cheer for the underdog. News organizations want people that cheer.

Conflict: Reporters are professional storytellers. All good stories have some kind of conflict. If you disagree with how the industry is being treated, you're more likely to receive coverage than if you agree.

Timely: Upcoming events, are often considered newsworthy.

There are many others. Think like the reporter. What is the "hook" in your story?

Start Writing
Press releases should be between 300 to 400 words. If it is a well-written press release, the reader should get the gist of it within the first two to three sentences. Spell-check the crap out of it! Do not just state the facts…tell a compelling story. You must find the balance between self-promotion and facts. Always make yourself available to any journalist who wants to use you as an honest source of information. Develop relationships with as many journalists as you can. Compelling images and informative graphics can add additional life to a press release if presented properly. You can also use a press release as a part of your crisis plan, should you ever run into any kind of trouble in your acting career. Sometimes defensive press releases are used to combat negative information in the press before it can become a crisis. Your career is a service-based business – never ruin your reputation or credibility. Let's hope that never happens.

23 Ideas for Press Releases

1. Any time you receive an award
2. When you sign with a talent manager
3. Inspirational stories related to your business
4. Media and speaker appearances
5. Milestones in your career
6. Adding or updating your website
7. Career anniversary
8. When projects are released
9. Any testimonials
10. When you sign with a talent agent
11. Inspirational stories
12. Any endorsement deals that you acquire
13. Being quoted in a book or article
14. Interviews on TV, radio, in a magazine or in a blog
15. Holiday-related events attended
16. Any merchandise release with your image
17. Any upcoming projects (only the information the filmmaker allows)
18. Pro bono work
19. Response to accusations against you
20. Piggyback off current news articles relating to the industry
21. Any meet and greets that you attend
22. Any charity events you attend
23. When projects are wrapped (only the information approved by the filmmaker)

Articles about You

Articles are kind of like press releases, with one major difference. Press releases are usually short lived. An article can hang around for quite some time.

There are 3 ways to get articles written about you.

- Do something so spectacular that the writer approaches you to get your story!
- You approach a writer with an angle for a story that their readers will benefit.
- Write and submit your own article.

You have decided to pursue your acting career. You want to be famous. In order to get famous...people need to know that you exist. Having someone write an article about you is one of the most credible ways to make that happen.

Here is a simple way to get the ball rolling. Connect journalists and let them know what you are about.

Until there is a buzz about you, you have to make your own buzz. So go out and ask for it! This is your business; YOU are the only one, right now, that is going to make it grow.

Use the Internet, phone book or a freakin' carrier pigeon to develop a list of journalists. Will they all respond favorably to you right now? NO! But keep plugging away! Make contacts, go to meet and greets and let them know that you are there and that you are awesome.

A slightly more difficult approach is to find out where your fan base gets their information about the industry. Is it a local news website, a blog or some other source? Contact the heads of those sources and say, "HEY, look at me. I've got a whole bunch of awesomeness for your readers!" Well, you probably do not want to say it that way, but you get the point.

Develop a list of potential journalists and follow them for a while. Read their articles. Follow them on social media. Share their articles on your social media sites. Create your own journalist database. Identify and develop relationships with the journalists who are most likely to help advance your career. Reach out to them. Don't pitch anything yet. Ask for advice. Be sincere. Develop the relationship. As the relationship develops, then see if they are interested on writing a story about you for your upcoming event.

Once you go for the pitch, make it easy for the journalist. Do not try and write an article and hand it to them. But it is okay to have jotted down some information about you, the event and a few quotes. NEVER ask them to do a profile piece on you. Right now, you do not have the fan base to support it.

Always go for the win-win. They are journalists – they like to write stories. They are not your personal cheerleader. Later in your career, when your awesomeness has paid off, hire them to be your personal cheerleader. But for now, let them do what they do best – write the story.

There are many reasons an actor might need to write a short biography. Websites, interviews, Press Releases, etc....

Here 4 guidelines for writing your Bio.

1. Make it short and sweet. Be direct, don't try to over impress.
2. Write it in third person. By title description, it is a biography, not an autobiography.
3. Don't list it out. Describe it. Describe your skills, training and experience in sentence form.
4. Include personal experiences. Give the article personality and a sense to connect.

There's really no wrong format for an acting bio. As long as you keep it in third person. It is important to talk about recent roles, any training and key parts of your personal life. A bio is not a resume. It is a short narrative that describes your story. It provides an opportunity to do a little bragging. It's also not a place to give an acceptance speech (makes you sound inexperienced and unprofessional). Tell your audience who you are as a person. You don't have to tell anything that you are not comfortable with disclosing.

Tips To Get Media to Write Articles about You

Step 1: Find The Right Journalist.
Use Google Reader and search for articles related to acting in your local area. Has some other actor in your area been the subject of an article? Who wrote the article? Contact them!

Step 2: Get The Journalist Motivated Enough To Write About You.
Send the journalist an email. Tell them why you are contacting them. Do not try to pitch them. Make it personal. Ask to meet them for advice. At the meeting, be honest, humble and tell them you are new to the acting industry and you are trying to make a name for yourself. Ask, in their opinion, how should you best use media sources to make that happen?

Step 3: Make It Worth It For Them.
Send them a follow-up email, thanking them for their time and input. If they write a story about you, write them a handwritten thank you card! They just did you a huge favor!

27 Ways to Get a Shot with the Media

1. Respond to a journalist's phone call or e-mail as soon as possible.
2. Don't cold call. Send an email first.
3. Congratulate them on their birthdays or other personal news they post.
4. Write a positive blog post highlighting a story they wrote (if you truly liked it).
5. Respond regularly to posts on their blog, if they have one.
6. Send an email or note a day after the interview thanking them for their time.
7. Stay on topic.
8. Offer to return as a regular guest or as needed, once your first interview concludes.
9. Leap on breaking news relevant to your industry.
10. Create a list of key dates, facts and quotes that are relevant to the story.
11. Give a two weeks' notice for an upcoming event.
12. Don't mail in information unsolicited.
13. Remain flexible in your schedule.
14. Express why this story is of value to your community.
15. Be excited about your event or story. If you are not excited, why should they be?
16. Build relationships months in advance of pitching.
17. Introduce yourself to journalists at meet and greets. REMEMBER: No pitching yet!
18. Assume anything you say will be printed.
19. Treat journalists with respect.
20. Invite journalists out for coffee and ask for advice…sincerely.
21. Talk in short sentences and avoid using slang or industry wording.
22. Don't show up in the newsroom unannounced.
23. Befriend the hosts of local radio talk shows in the same way you would a journalist.
24. If a journalist wants to interview you now, clear your schedule.
25. DO NOT say "no comment" if you can't answer a question. Explain why you can't.
26. When you pitch, focus on selling the benefits to the readers.
27. Link your story with a basic human emotion.

Chapter 8

How to Network in the Acting World

Chapter 8 How to Network in the Acting World

The following covers most of the networking opportunities that you will encounter. We are discussing what to do at the following:

- Meet & Greets
- Premieres
- Wrap Parties
- Release Parties
- Charity Events
- On Set
- Red Carpets

Meet & Greets

In the entertainment business you have to network. PERIOD.

Meet and Greets are parties and events that those within the industry attend to support the event, but also to network and make connections. These are so important. This is where you can connect with potential filmmakers, producers or other actors that may know of upcoming opportunities. You want to attend as many as possible, depending on who is going to be there, of course. If it is the same people over and over, it is not a benefit to you. However, when there are many to choose from with a large variety of industry representatives…BE THERE!

Having a solid network can provide awesome dividends in many different ways.

Taking a proactive approach to networking can truly help your acting career. It provides more than exchanging business cards. It means having an in-person physical connection to a person. It means the next time they email or talk to you on the phone there is now a connection that they would not have had if they had never met you.

Exchange contact information with everyone. You never know how someone you meet today can help you down the way. But you MUST be willing to help them as well. People are less likely to help you if they feel you are only out for yourself.

Realize that your true goals means you will need to build relationships with others. Building relationships requires networking, with a combination of offline and online.

I will guess that you spend more time on social media than you do in front of a camera. I will wager that you probably have social media friends that are powerhouses in the industry, but you have not met them in person. Change that. Pick 2 a week. Send a message to lead to an email to lead to a phone call. Let that lead to a true member of your network.

Now how do you network?

You need people to help you get to where you want to go. You need a way of identifying exactly if someone can or can't help you get there. You need a way to take strangers and turn them into acquaintances. Then you invite them to be part of your network. Of course, the ONLY way this is going to work is that if you expect them to help you – then you absolutely will help them.

Good networking is about giving and connecting to people to help them succeed. You do it for them. They do it for you.

To have a good network, you need a good plan. To have a good plan you need to set some goals.

Goals should be specific and measurable. Goals should be written down. I personally believe that you should get an accountability partner to help and motivate you to help you achieve your goals.

Goal Ideas:
- Get a talent manager
- Get an agent
- Add 3 influencers to my network this year
- Meet 10 film makers this year
- Attend a film festival
- Get new headshots
- Get your talent reel finished
- Be in 3 short films this year
- Be in at least 1 feature film this year

As you can see, all of these goals require that you know the right person. Now you have clearly set your goals and you know the specific people to help you achieve them. What if you do not currently know the people in each of these goals…? Then you got some work to do. Start networking!

Sometimes you meet the people you need by chance, sometimes you make it happen. Either way, always be ready to add them to your database of contacts. Include a brief note about how and when you met them. Then do your homework. Follow them on social media, look at their website and learn more about their recent and past projects.

If someone that you would like to add to your network will be at an upcoming event prepare a one page summary on them. Include topics that will help them connect to you.
I think it goes without saying….DON'T STALK ANYONE!

Start prior to the actual meet. Get on their radar by providing quality comments on the social media sites. Respectfully, send them any pertinent links about you. Tell them that you are attending the same event. Ask them to meet in person at the event.

People are usually very appreciative when you engage in this way.

Here are a few more thoughts on networking.

Email

NEVER SPAM! Only send emails that are full of quality content. Only send someone an email in the hopes of building your relationship with them.

Eating Out

Most folks eat 3 times a day. When you go out to do it, invite someone that you want to get deeper into your network (whoa, that sounded creepy), I mean someone that you would like to either add to your network or someone that you would like to professionally help out in some way. NOTICE – I said someone YOU can help. NOT them help you.

Meet & Greet / Wrap Party / Premiere Party

This is a prime time that is rich with opportunities to connect. You will not be able to have in depth conversations with everyone there. Make a goal to quality connect to 3-4 people. Have business cards, a smile and a firm but friendly handshake for everyone else.

Training Workshops

Do come prepared with business cards, pen and paper (the pen and paper is for contact information as well as notes). If possible try to find out everyone that will be there. Your number one goal should be to meet potential network contacts, make a connection and begin building a relationship.

So come prepared with insightful questions about their process and be well prepared with material that they request. Then, afterwards, stay in touch with all of your new network connections and continue to build your relationship with them.

Film Festivals / Conventions

These are great places to gain network connections. Hopefully you can gain a pretty good list of attendees and presenters. Do your homework on the ones you want to connect. Sometimes these events have a networking room….utilize it!

GET INVOLVED!

Premieres / Wrap / Release Parties / Charity Events

These are the heart and soul of a meet and greet. Go to these. Even though you may not be a part of this production, be there to support your fellow industry mates. Make sure, of course, that you are invited. These are not good parties to crash.

However, before you attend any such event. You should be prepared.

Your true purpose in going to an event like this is not having fun. It is not to have a chance to dress up. It is not to meet with old friends and make new ones. Yes, you can do all of those things while you are there, BUT, the true purpose is to advance your brand. Remember, you are an actor. Therefore, you are a business, so you should be there to promote and build your brand.

After all, as an outcome of attending this event you would like to get a meeting, audition, booking, etc…

So, now we have WHY we are doing it. The next question is HOW do we do it?

Simple. PREPARATION.

Now, we have been hanging out through quite a few pages. So, I feel I can trust you with a secret. (Looking both ways) I am scared to death of mingling at parties and events.

I can talk in front of a group of a thousand people and I am fine, but one on one. Ugh!

But, I had to beat it. So here are some of the tricks I learned.

Have an opening line. Have 2 or 3 different lines ready to use. And no, it can't be "Hi, my name is…"

It needs to be energetic. It needs to be sincere. You need to be upbeat. It needs to make the person you are talking to feel important, because they are. "Hello, it is so nice to finally meet you, I enjoy your work. My favorite is…" or "I have heard incredible things about your (agency, project, etc.). I hope you don't mind if I ask you a question about it?"

Be honest with it. Do not fake it. If you have to, practice in front of a mirror before the event to make sure the words don't stumble out, like I do.

People like to be appreciated. Most of the time, we all are impressed if someone is familiar with our work. It never hurts to make the other person smile.

Create an elevator speech.

An elevator speech is a 30 second statement that describes you the actor. It is informative. It is light hearted. But, most importantly, it is NOT boastful. Sum up your greatest achievements!

Include elements that make you:
- You never give an ordinary performance.
- You're easy to work with.
- You're marketable.

Here is a template:

"Hello, my name is _____ and I am currently working on a project called _____. I am working with an incredible cast and crew. I am truly excited with this project because of my passion for _____. So I know that it will be a major success!"

Write it out. Practice it as if it were a monologue. Perform it!

When you are in front of someone, understand that they may not be able to talk right then. If they are able to spend a few minutes to talk to you, listen to them. Don't wait for a pause to sell yourself. Show confidence. You have value.

Now the most important thing!

Know when to leave.

Come across as being totally awesome (because you are!) and move on. Mingle. Right now, you just want to give them a taste, not the whole meal. Besides, you are prepared. You have a list of other key people that you have to impress ☺

So, introduce yourself. Do your elevator speech. If things open up into a conversation, let it. If not – circulate. Have fun!

Walking the Red Capet

You step out of the limo. *Click, click, click* of the cameras. You are all decked out looking hot. You step out onto the red carpet. Fans are yelling your name. Spotlights are lighting up the nighttime skyline.

You know it sounds good to you. Otherwise you wouldn't be an actor.

Here are some thoughts on maximizing your red carpet experience.

Red Carpet Attitude. Study how other people react on Red Carpets. How do they walk? How do they pose? How do they carry themselves?

Know About the Event. Be prepared to answer questions about your past, current and upcoming projects. Share details about this event. Be confident.

Speak in Soundbites. When the powers that be edit all of the footage about the event, they will look for quick statements that get the point across quickly. Give them plenty to choose from.

Practice Posing. Practice, yes practice posing in the outfit you plan to wear in front of a full-length mirror. Do not just look at it from head on. Cameras can be anywhere around you. Look good from every angle. Or wear something else. Do each pose from different angles.

Practice Photos. Take pictures in your house, outside and in front of a lot of lights. How does the angle, light or shadows make you look? It is better to know now than to be surprised by looking in the after event photo galleries.

Do Practice Questions. Have someone ask possible questions. Practice your response. Your volume and tone. Where will you look? What pose will you do? Remember to speak in soundbites.

Trends. Know what is in style. Look hot for this year, not 1972. (I truly struggle with this one.) ☺

Learn from Your Past. Review what you have done in the past. Should you change your facial expression, your pose, your angle or your hair and make-up?

Enjoy yourself!

On Set

Sometimes, when you are on set you have seen people that are pushing their career or a screenplay to everyone there. Sometimes on set, you will come across those that have to tell you everything they have done. Let me be clear here: I am not putting those people down.

May I suggest instead of being the one that is doing all of the *talking*, be the one that is doing all of the *listening*. I am not saying to not say a word or to be uninviting. I am actually saying, be the one that everyone wants to approach to have a conversation.

Here is why. Take mental notes.

Who is talking about upcoming projects?
Who is the filmmaker on that project?
Who has access to the newest great agent?
Gather your info….do that recon.

Take the information, and if you can, fit it into your career strategy. Discuss what you learned with your agents and manager.

Meet & Greets / Premiere Parties / Wrap Parties / Release Parties

A meet and greet can be one of several different things. A party, a red carpet event, a film festival, a charity event, acting workshop or any place that people in the entertainment industry have gathered.

You have several goals at any of these:
- Find out who is attending (if possible)
- Of the people that could be there, whom do you need to develop an industry relationship
- Mingle
- Listen….you are still doing your recon
- Pass out your card to most
- Pass out your handout to your selected few

Your purpose for going to these meet and greets can be summed up in one word……..NETWORK.

Oh yes, parties. A chance to dress up, go out, have fun and forget your stress.

Yes, you can do those things while at industry parties, but that is not you primary purpose for going.

WHAT?

That is right, you have another purpose for going…to advance your career.

NO, I am not talking about going to an event and shoving your career plans down everyone's throats.

Yes, go have a great time. Yes, meet new people. Yes, connect with old friends. BUT, let's do some things to help advance your career while you are having fun. SAVVY?

Let's break it down into three major steps (with a few more minor steps).

Step 1. BEFORE THE EVENT
What is the purpose of this event?
Is it a red carpet, a wrap, or release party? Each requires you to work your brand!

Who will be at this event?
Press, filmmakers, executive producers, or influencers? If you know, make yourself a list of the guests that you must speak to and a list of whom you would like to speak to. Knock out both of these lists first, and then just have fun. Make sure you have business cards and handouts to pass out. REMEMBER, do not be pushy. You are an actor, not a used car salesperson. Have fun. Mingle.

What is the layout of this event?
Is there a red carpet or a banner? Will your picture be taken? Is it indoors or outdoors? Keep this in mind when deciding how you dress. Dress accordingly. Let people remember you because you were a pleasure to be around, not because the wind blew up your flowing dress or that color black you were wearing looked see-through when pictures were taken.

Step 2. DURING THE EVENT
In this order:
- Your introductions to the host (and if there is anyone they want to introduce to you).
- Speak to the guests on your MUST TALK TO list. Give cards and handouts. Be cool.
- Get a drink and light snack.
- Speak to the guests on your LIKE TO TALK list. Give cards. Still be cool.
- Mingle/eat/dance/have fun.

Step 3. AFTER THE EVENT
While you were at the event, you collected business cards from those around you. You took mental notes of upcoming projects. You developed the basics of some friendships. Now follow up on all of that. Make your calls, add people to your social media pages, send out the thank you's and contact the powers that be that want you for an upcoming project. Make sure to contact your agent and manager – Kaleigh Group Entertainment (shameless plug) – on how it went.

Charity Events

Attending a charity event can be fun and rewarding. There are many charities that do a lot of good in their communities. Support them! I am not suggesting that you exploit them. No one should ever do that. What I am suggesting is to capitalize on what you do in good taste.

For our purposes right now, we are going to treat a charity event similar to a Meet and Greet.

No matter if you are building a home, working in a soup kitchen, or attending a fundraiser, these are great things!

Attend it, work hard at it, have fun at it…to advance your career.

Again, let's be clear: the biggest difference is at the charity event you are there to help more than you are to advance your career. You will not make any attempt to shove your career down anyone's throat. (I know you knew that, but just had to say it to make sure.☺) As far as advancing your career we shall be very subtle, but with purpose.

Yes. There are three steps here as well.

Step 1. BEFORE THE EVENT
Is it a working or relaxing event?
Are you going to be building, cooking, cleaning or any other type of work? Or is this an event where you can dress up, have dinner, drinks, etc…? Dress accordingly as to how your brand fits into the event.

Speak with the organizer of the event.
Confirm that it is okay to have someone come by and take action pictures of you for publicity purposes. Ensure that you will meet their guidelines (no publishing people's faces without their permission, show proprietary or trade secret information, etc…) Explain how the photos will be used if they ask.

Line up your photographer?
What?! No, you are not going to do a photo shoot. You are just going to have someone come by and take a few shots of you as you are working or attending. The idea here is to get an action shot of you helping… We are going to use this picture later for Press Releases.

What is the layout of this event?
Indoors? Outdoors? Are you getting dirty or are you dressed up? How many people will be there? I know it sounds crazy, but remember this: the pictures that you take are how your potential fans SEE your career develop in front of them. Each picture taken needs to look professional and complimentary to your career.

Step 2. DURING THE EVENT
In this order:
- Work hard.
- Do great work for the charity.
- Get your photo taken without any disruption to the event.
- Politely and friendly answer questions as to why you are getting your picture taken.
- Develop new friendships from the inquisitive people that ask you questions.
- Have fun!

Step 3. AFTER THE EVENT
Follow up with the organizer to thank them for the opportunity. Discuss the idea if there is any way that through your acting is there any way to show additional support to their charity. Do they need a spokesperson? Can you connect them to any filmmaker friends to do a public service announcement, etc.? Take the best pictures that you took and add them to a press release that discusses you wanting to give back to your community. Something along the lines of "Their career is built on make-believe, but their heart is real for the community..." You get the idea.

While you were there, you probably met a lot of great people. You developed some new friendships. Enjoy those.

Chapter 9
Building Your Entourage

Chapter 9   Building Your Entourage

This is your career. This is your business. YOU, the actor, are the business. The responsibility of making your name a household name falls on your shoulders or those that you partner with (that have the ability to do so).

If you were hanging from a cliff, would you want to do so by one finger or all ten? The more there are, the stronger, smarter and more efficient you become.

Teams are important…but you already know that.

Below are the different sets of members you need on your team. Do you pay them? Probably don't have that kind of cash just lying around right now! Unless you can afford it – then do so. You will probably not have the money to start. Some will partner with you on a commission basis (agent and manager); others you can pay by exchanging services, notoriety or just being a friend and doing the same for them.

TALENT AGENTS

According to Wikipedia, the free encyclopedia, a Talent Agent, or Booking Agent, is:

> *A person who finds jobs for actors, authors, film directors, musicians, models, film producers, professional athletes, writers, screenwriters, broadcast journalists, and other people in various entertainment or broadcast businesses.*

Did you catch that? They are a booking agent. Their job is NOT to make you famous. Their job is to book you work.

I want to point this out, because most talent agents are very hardworking and do their best to book work for their talent.

They will probably help you out in every way that they can and have time for. But here is the problem – they are not set up to market you, just to book you. Most just simply do not have the time to do it.

I am in no way putting down agents. I think their job is tough and tedious, but they get it done. They are awesome!

Some focus in different parts of the industry. They may be geographic, genre, reality, etc. So, keep that in mind. You may need more than one. Entire books are written on choosing the best agents for you. This is not one of those books. My purpose here is to stress to you that you MUST develop a very active and mutual relationship with them. Keep them up to date on any physical or address changes.

You need to be a sellable product. If you haven't worked, have no type of training or no one has ever heard of you…it will be difficult for an agent to sign you. Get work, be in student films and take some workshops. Give the talent agent something that they can use to get you in front of filmmakers and casting directors.

Here are a few things to keep in mind when getting an agent:

Legitimate talent agents have to be licensed by the state in which they work. Talent managers require no such license.

It is important to find a talent agent and talent manager you can easily relate to and who understands your acting goals.

Just like any industry, there are good and bad. Choose the right agent and manager for you.

Be careful of agents and managers that put their own acting career in front of yours. It is okay for them to act, but they are representing you. If they do not put you first, choose someone who will.

Talent agents hate to deal with divas…DON"T BE ONE, I don't care how big you get. Nobody likes a diva.

Communicate often with your agent and manager. Good agents and managers want you to be successful. Help them help you be successful!

Develop a truly professional relationship with your agent. Stay in touch with them. Check several times a day your email (that you set up just for casting notices) from them. We all know how an emergency casting may need to be filled right now. When they want a video submission, do not wait until the last second to get it to them. You are a professional – always act like it.

BUILD YOUR ENTOURAGE

Talent Managers

A Talent Manager and a Talent Agent are not the same thing. For the purposes of this book, we promised each other that we would keep it simple. As previously mentioned, a Talent Agent books roles for you the actor. A Talent Manager is responsible for the development of your career. This may include contract negotiations, merchandise development, public relations, financial control and so much more. Some would argue that when an actor is just starting out, there is not as much of a need for a Talent Manager. I do not follow that course. I believe, just like you do, that your career needs to be constantly built from day one!

Here are some things to keep in mind when signing with a Talent Manager:

A good talent manager will be focused on trying your build your career.

A talent manager will work WITH your agents to help ensure your success.

Just like when choosing an agent, can you work with the manager? Do you think you will get along? Does the business relationship feel right?

Again, DON'T BE A DIVA!

No talent agent or talent manager should ever ask for any money up front. If they say you need to "give us $500 and we will make you famous," you need to look them in the face and say, "I don't think so!" Then run away! (Don't trot...I said RUN!).

Have trust in them. Have patience, and let them do their job. If you are new to acting, it will take some time to build your career. Don't call them up and say, "I know I started my acting career last Thursday, but why haven't you made me famous yet?"

Communicate often with your talent manager.

Is it imperative that you have a manager? No. However, do you want to take the necessary time to learn how and execute your marketing plan to advance your career? If you do, there is nothing wrong with that. But it doesn't hurt to have an expert in your corner. That would be me! (Shameless plug!☺)

If you choose to have a manager…again, cultivate a positive working relationship. Everything that I (and other managers in the industry) do for clients is to build their career. It truly helps when they understand that and provide the things I ask for in a timely manner. Sometimes, because of deadlines or sudden opportunities, a request may seem strange or inconvenient, but the mission is simple: to advance the career of the client.

Talent managers focus on managing an actor's career. Talent managers handle public relations for the actor, the business side of acting for the actor, and work with the actor on planning the success of an actor's career. They typically work with their clients over a period of a number of years. They protect the actor.

Here is a quick list of some of the duties talent managers do for their clients:

- Prepare the acting resume for the talent.
- Advise talent on acting workshops, classes and coaching.
- Assist in any and all decisions related to the talent's career.
- Promote talent to industry professionals.
- Help the talent network.
- Arrange introductions to talent agents.
- Help talent in choosing a photographer for headshots.

Talent managers assist with accurately listing their talent on IMDb, Actors Access, and other key acting sites. Additionally, talent managers can assist talent with their membership in SAG-AFTRA and other acting unions.

By law, unless a talent manager has the appropriate state licensing, they cannot legally find their clients any work. That is why talent managers work so hard with reputable talent agents (because they are licensed to get the actor the work). Typically, both talent agents and talent managers each receive a fifteen to twenty percent commission.

PUBLIC RELATIONS FIRM
According to the Book of Ron...page two (that means this is my own personal definition), a public relations firm is the following:

> *A Public Relations Firm (Publicist) is a professional company that provides a service which is geared towards identifying, catering and modifying a plan to build you up.*

Public relations firms are experts in developing plans to make the public (your audience) feel and think about you in a predetermined way. That is what they do. That is all they do. They are experts on that subject.

Simply put, public relation firms can be expensive. They can probably do a very nice job in creating a plan for you. You will, of course, have to pay for that expensive plan, up front. If you have the financial ability to do that, then please utilize their expertise.

Hopefully, there will be a time when you need to hire a publicist to do your promotion for you.

Publicity requires a plan. It is not something that can just be done overnight. You must have the press kit, collection of materials and schedule of releases. If they're in a film, you want to have a six-month lead-time to put the media list together and tailor it to the target audience.

With a PR firm, be prepared to pay up front, rather than a commission. A PR firm can range anywhere from $1000 to $5000 per month plus expenses. Expenses can include: travel, photographer, supplies, postage, etc.

Sometimes you can utilize the PR firm that is part of a project that you are working with for free.

Just remember there is no point in hiring a publicist until there is something worth publicizing! As an actor, you only need to hire a publicist when you have a story to tell. Don't let your ego get in the way, just so that you can say you have a publicist. If you have a lot of bookings, then go crazy and hire a great one! A publicist can make sure your face is out there, that you get out to premieres, get photographed and create a buzz around you.

What Publicists Do
They assist with seeking and arranging charity appearances, red carpet events, press kit, press releases and articles. The great ones will even train you on how to do interviews, what to say and not say and how to be interesting. They sometimes accompany you to red carpet events to introduce you to the RIGHT media folks. They have even gone so far as to handle fan mail, websites and message boards.

How to Make Your Publicist's Job Easier

- Return calls in a timely manner – publicity is usually time sensitive.
- Show up for interviews.
- Publicists are professionals – treat them that way.

YOU

Well, my friend that is where this book comes in. That is where the resources you gain from this book, your own research and input from others in the acting industry come together to give you the knowledge you need to develop your own plan.

Decide exactly what you are looking for from this industry.

How Famous Do You Want To Be?
Some people are happy with just being a background actor or an extra. Some people want to go all of the way. Obviously, the higher you want to go, the harder it will be to get there. Are you up for it?

How Deep Into This Are You Willing To Go?
There will be many phone calls, hours of searching, castings in low- or no-pay gigs to get closer to that big one, many networking opportunities to get the right contacts, and workshops to increase your skill as an actor. Are you up for it?

How Much Effort Can You Honestly Put Into Your Acting Career?
Chances are you have a day job right now. If you do, great! That means you are taking care of you and yours. I respect that. But the question is…how do you pursue your acting career with your current responsibilities. Only you can answer that.

What Resources Do You Have Available To You To Reach Your Goals?
This book, the Internet, multiple organizations, other actors, film schools and so many more!

These are a few more members that you should strongly consider adding to your team:

Megaphone Team

This is your personal team. These are friends and fellow members of the acting industry that you have brought together. The purpose of this team is simple – to advance all of your careers. They do this for you; you, in return, do it for them.

When you post a press release, picture, or video on your social media pages, you like and share it.
When you hear of an upcoming event, you tell each other.
When you hear of an upcoming project, you tell each other.
When you need a testimony, you give it to each other.
When you learn of something that can advance your career, you share it with each other.

Crew for Headshots, Website, Filming Auditions and Editing Actor Reels

These are the technical people of your team. If you are a technology nerd, good for you. You can probably do most of this yourself. However, the rest of us are going to need the expertise of a great photographer, someone to run your website, someone to help in filming your auditions and someone to put together your actor reel. All of these team members are needed.

Remember, you have got to make the first impression the right impression.

Fans

This is the fun one. This one is the purpose of all of your hard work. You tell yourself: I act because I love the art. Go ahead; you believe that…I don't. You, just like me, just like every other actor out there…we do it for the recognition. We do it for ego. Not faulting anyone, just stating the truth.

These last 2 team members YOU MUST OBTAIN!

Why?

Because, they are going to help you get in front of a lot of people at one time. These two have followers that listen to them and do what they say.

Connecting with Industry Bloggers

In my opinion, one of the best ways to gain notoriety, buzz, fame or whatever you want to call it is having multiple people who write blogs (bloggers) talk about you.

Blogs are everywhere. They are easy to start and gain followers. Think of them as mini magazines or newspapers.

To me, it makes total sense that if a blogger already has a following of people. Why shouldn't you capitalize on it!

You don't have to take the time to build the community…they have already done it.

But if you're going to succeed, you need to build strong relationships with bloggers who believe in you talent and want to help advance your acting career. This takes work. It is not just sending off a few emails.

The good news is that there are proven ways to make your blogger outreach a success.

Online blogger introduction sites are a great way of finding bloggers. Bloggers on these sites are already interested in connecting, so you're more likely to get a better response than if you just send out cold-calling emails.

Some kind of product giveaway is a great tool to get bloggers to focus on you. Free classes, autographed photos, free DVDs, etc... Don't try to control what a blogger says about you.

Ask them for feedback on your website, blog, performance, etc. Show them that you value their opinion. You'll benefit as well. They know their audience (your potential community and fan base). They are providing you with insight to what that audience wants.

They will also be looking for ways to expand their audience. So, promote them on your social media sites, web site and press releases.

If it is all possible meet with them face to face. More than likely you will only have an online relationship with them, but if possible get to know them face to face.

No one likes being used. If you only get in contact when you want them to write a post, you're going to turn them off very quickly. Snail mail them a thank you note. Show your appreciation.

Stay in touch with them. Build the relationship with them.

Don't Get Stingy With The Comments. Every blogger likes getting comments. It is nice to know that somebody is reading your content and leaving their thoughts. One way to get the attention of some fellow bloggers and build your brand is to leave comments on other peoples' blogs. And please, DON'T SPAM and leave real quality comments!

Social Media Endorsers

Here is my personal definition of an influencer:

> *People that are within an industry who have a very large following and whose followers trust what they have to say about that industry.*

Why Is This Type Of Person Important To You?
Simple. Would you rather take the time to build a relationship with ten thousand potential fans, OR would you rather have one person bring you those ten thousand fans? I doubt that you have the time it takes to build a rapport and then a relationship with ten thousand potential fans.

Why Does Your Brand Need an Influencer?
Consumers trust recommendations from third parties more than any other type of marketing. That is why. An influencer is someone your potential fan base already trusts. Because of the loyalty of their audience, an influencer has the ability to increase your social media exposure and flat-out sell you to your potential fan base!

Where to Look for Influencers:
Social Media Monitoring
Look for those that like or follow your comments and actions on social media. Connect with them. Get them excited to become a brand advocate. These are like personal cheerleaders. Stay focused on your social media mentions and blog posts about your brand – "YOU, the actor" – and you will find influencers and advocates you didn't realize you had.

Additionally, social media monitoring allows you to find influencers who advocate for acting in your area. Connect with them. You have a common interest – acting in your community.

Google Alerts
Set alerts for keywords pertaining to your brand – "YOU the actor" – and acting in your community. Identify anyone who is actively posting about it.

Blogger Outreach
Connect with lead bloggers that discuss acting in your community. Build a rapport and business relationship with them.

Encourage Content Creation
A true influencer of your brand is passionate about YOU, the actor, or at least acting in your community. Capitalize on that passion. Make it your personal goal to get as much content to them as they can handle. Give them insight, interviews, statistics or anything else that you have that could help them do what they love…blogging about their subject.

Compensate Influencers
If someone is going to say good things about you, they need to be compensated. It doesn't have to be money. It can be an invitation to a meet and greet, a DVD of your latest work or anything like that of value. The point is you want the influencer to feel rewarded.

Lastly, connecting with influencers does take time. Earn their attention through your awesomeness. You've got this!

Chapter 10
Buzz Building Blueprint

Chapter 10   Buzz Building Blueprint

This is it. This is your plan!

Over the course of the next year complete these tasks.

When you have finished this blue print you will have:

- Created your Brand
- Created Your Elevator pitch
- Determined if you need a Mentor to guide you
- Created key industry related accounts
- Submit an Article about you to 5 different sites
- Submit 12 press releases about you to different sites
- Have your Website and social media sites in several Directories
- Have a Talent Agent and a Talent Manager (if you want them)
- Have done 4 Interviews
- Attended 1 Charity Events
- Attended 4 Meet & Greets
- Attended 1 Premiere / Wrap / Release Party
- Attended 1 Red Carpet
- Created a Blog
- Created a Website
- Created a Press Kit
- Created your Social Media Pages
- Created your Business Cards
- Created your Handouts / Postcards
- Created your Actor Reel
- Connect with 5 Social Media Endorsers
- Connect with 3 Industry Bloggers

AND SO MUCH MORE...

Figure out who you are as an actor

___ **Complete the TYPE Worksheet**

___ **Complete the Create Your Brand Worksheet**

Now shorten your description.

Create Your Elevator pitch
Make sure it is:
___ *Telling a Short Story.* A beginning, middle and end.
___ *Concise.* Your time limit is 30-60 seconds.
___ *Targeted.* Make it specific to the listener.
___ *Clear.* Use simple words. Make it easy to follow.
___ *Visual.* Use words that create a visual image in their mind.
___ *Having a Hook.* Catch their attention and keep it.
___ *Goal Oriented.* What is the purpose of giving the pitch? Audition, representation, etc.?

Do you need a Mentor to guide you?

Create a list from people you have or would like to work with on a project.

Who is someone you respect?
List 3 people:

_____

_____

_____

Have they already gone down the path that you have chosen?

Do they possess knowledge that you want?

Will they be brutally honest with you?

Who do I contact to reach a potential mentor?

Name _____

Contact Info _____

Create an account:

      800 Castings
User name:_____ Pw:_____

      Actor's Access
User name:_____ Pw:_____

      IMDb
User name:_____ Pw:_____

Press:

___ Write an introductory article about yourself

___ Submit Article to 5 different sites

    Date _____
    Site _____

    Date _____
    Site _____

    Date _____
    Site _____

    Date _____
    Site _____

    Date _____
    Site _____

___ Write introductory press release about you

___ Submit press release to 5 different sites

    Site _____

    Site _____

    Site _____

    Site _____

    Site _____

___ Submit Website and social media sites to 5 Directories

    Site _____

    Site _____

    Site _____

    Site _____

    Site _____

Contact:

___ Try to obtain a Talent Agent

Name	Contact Info	Result
Name	Contact Info	Result
Name	Contact Info	Result

___ Try to obtain a Talent Manager

Name	Contact Info	Result
Name	Contact Info	Result
Name	Contact Info	Result

___ Set up 4 Interviews

Name	Contact Info	Result
Name	Contact Info	Result
Name	Contact Info	Result
Name	Contact Info	Result

Attend:
___ 1 Charity Event

Event:
_____

Location:
_____

Date: _____   Time: _____

Event Purpose:
_____

Goal 1:
_____

Goal 2:
_____

Goal 3:
_____

___ 4 Meet & Greets

    Event #1: _____

    Location: _____

    Date: _____   Time: _____

    Host: _____

    Goal: _____

    Key Contact: _____

    ___ Snail Mailed Host Thank You Note after event

    Event #2: _____

    Location: _____

    Date: _____   Time: _____

    Host: _____

    Goal: _____

    Key Contact: _____

    ___ Snail Mailed Host Thank You Note after event

Event #3:
_____

Location:
_____

Date: _____   Time: _____

Host:
_____

Goal:
_____

Key Contact:
_____

___ Snail Mailed Host Thank You Note after event

Event #4:
_____

Location:
_____

Date: _____   Time: _____

Host:
_____

Goal:
_____

Key Contact:
_____

___ Snail Mailed Host Thank You Note after event

___ 1 Premiere / Wrap / Release Party

    Event:
    _____

    Location:
    _____

    Date: _____ Time: _____

    Host:
    _____

    Goal:
    _____

    Key Contact:
    _____

    ___ Snail Mailed Host Thank You Note after event

___ 1 Red Carpet

    Event:
    _____

    Location:
    _____

    Date: _____ Time: _____

    Host:
    _____

    Goal:
    _____

    Key Contact:
    _____

    ___ Snail Mailed Host Thank You Note after event

Develop:

Blog

___ Setup blog through Blogger

Blog Musts:
___ Write 2-3 blog posts each week
___ Share blog posts on Facebook, Twitter, Google+ and LinkedIn
___ Subscribe to 2 new blog feeds weekly
___ Create a way to track your followers
___ Create a content schedule.

Blogging Ideas:
- Upcoming events
- Upcoming projects (with proper permissions)
- Projects you recently finished
- How you got started
- Questions from fans
- Experiences and challenges
- Lessons that you have learned
- A day in your life
- Audition experiences
- Meet-and-greet experience

Keep in Mind:
___ Keep paragraphs short
___ Add pictures whenever you can
___ Encourage fans to leave comments
___ Connect your posts with Google Authorship and other blog directories.
___ Make sure your website, social media pages and blog are connected
___ Make sure fans can easily subscribe to your blog

Website

Pages that you should include:
1. **Welcome Page.** Include a headshot that portrays the "real you."
2. **Blog.** Write in a personal format.
3. **Headshots.** Have several different looks.
4. **Resume.** Number one rule….KEEP IT UP TO DATE!
5. **Bio.** Introduce yourself. Highlight your career. Include testimonials. Include your training.
6. **Actor Reel.** Make your career experience look like a hot trailer from a hit movie ☺
7. **Social Media Links.** Twitter, Facebook Fan Page, LinkedIn, Stage 32, Instagram, etc.
8. **Photo Gallery.** Include promotional, behind-the-scenes, etc.
9. **A Business Email.** The ONLY thing you use it for is to build your career.

Press Kit

Items needed for a Press Kit:
1. Pictures of you. Headshots with different looks.
2. Any articles written about you.
3. Any projects that you are currently working on.
4. Any charity work you are currently involved with.
5. Include contact information for your Website and social media.
7. Your biography.
8. Any Endorsements.

Press Release

Topic of Press Release:
Who_____

What_____

Where_____

When_____

How_____

Why_____

Parts of a Press Release

Contact information in the top left hand corner of the page.

Skip a line.

Sometimes you need to have your story released immediately. If so type:
FOR IMMEDIATE RELEASE/To Be Released on XX/XX/XX

Other times you might have a little time. If so provide the date it needs to be released.

Skip a line.

Four or Five word Headline.

Skip a line.

Location of where your news is taking place, followed by a dash (-), the date and another dash. For example:

"Raleigh, NC – 19 July 2015 –"

Skip a line.

WHO, WHAT, WHERE, WHEN, WHY and HOW.

Skip a line.

Your contact information.

Skip a line.

Secondary details. Should expand on the first paragraph.

Then 3 number signs ### centered at the bottom of the page

Helpful Tips and Reminders

- Outline it before you write.
- Keep it simple.
- Be brief, positive and specific.
- Be accurate.
- Don't repeat yourself.
- Proof read and spell check.
- Proof read and spell check again.
- Have it to them at the START of the business day.
- Send it to multiple sites.
- Don't be surprised if they do not run it.

Articles about You

___ Do something so spectacular that the writer approaches you to get your story!

___ You approach a writer with an angle for a story that their readers will benefit.

___ Write and submit your own article.

___ Find out where your fan base gets their information about the industry.

Potential Journalists
___ Develop a list of potential journalists
___ Read their articles
___ Follow them on social media
___ Share their articles on your social media sites
___ Reach out to them
___ Ask for advice
___ Be sincere
___ Develop the relationship

27 Ways to Get a Shot with the Media

1. Respond to a journalist's phone call or e-mail as soon as possible.
2. Don't cold call. Send an email first.
3. Congratulate them on their birthdays or other personal news they post.
4. Write a positive blog post highlighting a story they wrote (if you truly liked it).
5. Respond regularly to posts on their blog, if they have one.
6. Send an email or note a day after the interview thanking them for their time.
7. Stay on topic.
8. Offer to return as a regular guest or as needed, once your first interview concludes.
9. Leap on breaking news relevant to your industry.
10. Create a list of key dates, facts and quotes that are relevant to the story.
11. Give a two weeks' notice for an upcoming event.
12. Don't mail in information unsolicited.
13. Remain flexible in your schedule.
14. Express why this story is of value to your community.
15. Be excited about your event or story. If you are not excited, why should they be?
16. Build relationships months in advance of pitching.
17. Introduce yourself to journalists at meet and greets. REMEMBER: No pitching yet!
18. Assume anything you say will be printed.
19. Treat journalists with respect.
20. Invite journalists out for coffee and ask for advice…sincerely.
21. Talk in short sentences and avoid using slang or industry wording.
22. Don't show up in the newsroom unannounced.
23. Befriend the hosts of local radio talk shows in the same way you would a journalist.
24. If a journalist wants to interview you now, clear your schedule.
25. DO NOT say "no comment" if you can't answer a question. Explain why you can't.
26. When you pitch, focus on selling the benefits to the readers.
27. Link your story with a basic human emotion.

Social Media Pages

When your followers try to engage with you, respond!
DO NOT use your social media to oversell yourself.
Build rapport.

Building Your Social Media Strategy
Build a fan page.
Do not use your personal pages for acting.
Take a very methodical approach.
Create fan pages for the sole purpose of promoting your acting career.
Post between 11am to 10pm.
Make sure you use the right language and tags.
Make sure that all of your profiles stay up to date.
Always remember that social media is part of your overall self-promotion campaign

Facebook
___ Publish 3 updates daily
___ Link it to your blog posts
___ Monitor for comments; reply as needed

Twitter
___ Publish 5-6 tweets daily, including your blog posts
___ Retweet 3-5 relevant tweets daily
___ Retweet influencers
___ Respond to tweets
___ Follow new people everyday

LinkedIn
___ Publish 5-6 updates daily
___ Participate in industry groups 2-3 times weekly
___ Like or comment on 3 pieces of content daily
___ Scan industry groups a few times a week
___ Connect with 5 new people weekly

Google+
___ Publish 3 updates daily, including your blog posts
___ Use Circles to create relevant connections
___ Add 10-15 people to circles weekly
___ Make sure your posts are public

YouTube
___ Create a video of your monologues
___ Ensure that your Talent Reel is visible
___ Post a new video weekly
___ Ask questions from fans and create videos to address them
___ Add fun in your videos
___ Use a videographer for events that you attend

Business Cards

___ MUST look professional
___ It must impress the person receiving it
___ MUST have a picture of you on it. After all, YOU are the brand!
___ Keep the cards on you
___ Plan to give out "X" amount of cards to key people

Just give it to the people that will benefit your career.

Business cards are not going to get you work! They connect you to people who can.

Handouts / Postcards

Around four by six inches
On the front are your name, full body, the quarter body shot and a headshot
On the back is a quick resume of the acting work that you have done

___ Use them along with a press release to casting agents and filmmakers.

___ Send them to fans about upcoming roles.

___ Send them to agents and managers that you want to sign.

___ Design it to fit the genre.

___ Use a P.O. Box, your agent's, or manager's address. Never use your personal addresses.

___ If you are going to use someone else's likeness, make sure that you have permission.

___ Send postcards out about every 2 months.

ALWAYS, ALWAYS, ALWAYS make yourself look good!

Actor Reel

__ Video yourself performing monologues.
__ Act out a scene with other actors.
__ Have someone interview you.
__ Get with some actor friends and create a short film (for the sole purpose of filming you).

You can do it from a good mobile device on a tripod (not hand held).

As you get more work, substitute until you have the best reel in the industry.

Put it on your:
    Website
    Industry sites
    Your social media pages

Remember, the final product is going to make your first impression

Choose (or make) a scene that provides you in a good light.

Make sure the sound is good.

Hand Out Your Face Attitude

YOU have to go out there and make this work.
YOU have got to lead your team to help you be more successful.
YOU have got to be the driving force behind your success.

Most importantly...
    YOU have got to believe in yourself.
    YOU have got to know YOU are worth the recognition.
    YOU have got to know that you are good enough.
    YOU have got to know that you are worthy.
    YOU have got to stay focused.
    YOU must persevere!

Headshots

Make sure that there is expression in your eyes.

It is called a headshot; make sure it is a shot of your head.

It should never focus on a "cool" background.

Have a simple clear photo with a neutral background.

It should be a shoulders and above shot.

Your shoulders should be squared off to camera, not turned away.

The camera should be level with your eyes.

Don't have your hands on your face.

Try to get the reflection of the lights in your eyes.

NEVER EVER touchup your headshot.

Resume

What do they want to see on your resume?

- Your successes
- Production companies you have worked with
- Characters you've played
- Directors and producers you've worked with
- Teachers you've had
- Special skills
- Credits that stand out

(A guest star role on a network show carries more weight than one on an unknown web series)

Keep your resume crisp and clean so that our eyes go straight to the most important details.

Put your credits by and large in chronological order.

If you do not yet have any impressive credits, focus on training that you have had.

KEEP IT UP TO DATE. KEEP IT UP TO DATE. KEEP IT UP TO DATE.

Create relationship:

___ 5 Social Media Endorsers

Name	Contact Info	Result
Name	Contact Info	Result
Name	Contact Info	Result
Name	Contact Info	Result
Name	Contact Info	Result

___ 3 Industry Bloggers

Name	Contact Info	Result
Name	Contact Info	Result
Name	Contact Info	Result

Additional To Do List:

While On Set develop networking contacts.
Send out monthly Thank you Cards.

Quarterly
        Attend Event
        Guest Blog

Annually
        Attend Workshop
        Review Website
        Review Blog
        Review Social Media Site

Chapter 11
Resources

Chapter 11　　　　　　　　　　　　Resources

Let's Get Started!

33 Ways to Market YOU, the Actor

1. Create a presence, post video, share links, share articles and comment daily on Facebook.
2. Get interviewed by other websites or blogs.
3. Respond to free PR opportunities offered by HARO (Help-A-Reporter-Out).
4. Create a presence, post videos, share links, articles and comment three times daily on Twitter.
5. Publish a video with your personality on YouTube.
6. Post comments on other related blogs.
7. Ask for and give recommendations on LinkedIn.
8. Create a presence, post video, share links, share articles and comment daily on LinkedIn
9. Have an Actors Access membership.
10. Have 800 castings membership.
11. Create a presence, post video, share links, share articles and comment daily on Stage32.
12. Have a proper and professional headshot.
13. Attend up to 4 seminars in the first year.
14. Create a presence and post your video; also comment daily on your own blog.
15. Always, Always, Always keep your acting resume up to date.
16. Review your career plan and adjust as needed.
17. Have business cards at all times.
18. Create a funny and a dramatic monologue.
19. Develop YOUR Brand.
20. Create your own talent website.
21. List your website with directories and maximize the Search Engine Optimization. Update it often.
22. Create an email with a signature. Use it for ALL and ONLY acting communication with your links.
23. Set up an IMDb page.
24. Always do a New Project Press Release.
25. Attend a few of the red carpet events throughout the year.
26. Review Casting List daily.
27. You should attend at least two talent-training workshops per year.
28. When you sign with a new agent or manager do a Sign-On Press Release.
29. Whenever you have a new video (monologues, auditions, etc.) put it on your YouTube channel.
30. Send out a press release at least once a month.
31. Work in PSA projects.
32. Work in projects in student films if you are starting out to develop experience and contacts.
33. Work in projects in the background if you are starting out to develop experience and contacts.

PUSH / PULL / CONTENT
Marketing Check List

Actor Web Sites to Join
___ *Actor's Access*
___ *800 Castings*
___ *IMDb*
___ *Directories*

Team Members to Get
___ *Talent Agents*
___ *Talent Managers*
___ *Megaphone Team*

Activities to Do
___ *Get Business Cards*
___ *Get Handouts*
___ *Go to Meet & Greets*
___ *Attend Premieres / Wrap / Release Parties*
___ *Get Cast for Public Service Announcements*
___ *Set Up Speaking Engagements*
___ *Attend Charity Events*
___ *Get Your Own Website*
___ *Develop Contacts When You Are On Set*
___ *Create and Maintain Your Social Media Pages*
___ *Create and Maintain Your Blog*
___ *Get Press Releases Written About You*
___ *Get Articles Written About You*
___ *Develop a Relationship with Social Media Influencers*
___ *Attend Red Carpet Events*
___ *Get Interviewed*

WHAT TO LOOK FOR IN AN AGENT AND MANAGER

A talent agent (in most states) must be licensed by the state.

What is the commission rate of the talent agent?

A talent manager does usually not have to be licensed by the state.

What is the commission rate of the talent manager?

If you are a member of SAG/AFTRA, the agreement MUST meet their guidelines.

What is the length of the term?

Exactly what is the coverage of the agreement?

Is the agreement exclusive or non-exclusive?

Is there an allowance for Carve OUTS?

Is there a "package fee"?

Is the agent or manager requesting any upfront fees?

Does the agent or manager receive a commission on travel expenses paid to you?

MEET & GREETS / PARTIES
Check List

Step 1. BEFORE THE EVENT
What is the purpose of this event?
Is it a red carpet, a wrap or release party? Each requires you to work your brand!

Who will be at this event?

> *Press*
> *Filmmakers*
> *Executive Producers*
> *Influencers*
> *Other* _____

Who are the people you MUST talk to?
1. _____
2. _____
3. _____

Who are the people you would LIKE TO talk to?
1. _____
2. _____
3. _____

What is the layout of this event?
Is there a red carpet, a banner, etc.? Will your picture be taken? Is it indoors/outdoors? Keep this in mind for how you dress. Dress accordingly.

Step 2. DURING THE EVENT
___ Meet with and thank the host for your invitation.
___ Scope, approach and speak with your MUST talk list.
___ Scope, approach and speak with your LIKE TO talk list.
___ Have plenty of business cards and handouts available.
___ Have fun.

Step 3. AFTER THE EVENT
___ Collect contact information from others.
___ Add connections to your social media pages.
___ Remember something about them that you can recount later.
___ Follow up with them at the appropriate time.
___ Send a handwritten thank you to the host for inviting you.

CHARITY EVENTS
Check List

Step 1. BEFORE THE EVENT
Is it a working or relaxing event?
Are you going to be building, cooking, cleaning or any other type of work? Or is this an event where you can dress up, have dinner, drinks, etc.? Dress accordingly as to how your brand fits into the event.

Will the organizer allow for your photo taken for publicity purposes?

Line up your photographer!
Date:
Time:
Place:
Entrance:
Type of Shot:
Surroundings:
Others Attending:

Step 2. DURING THE EVENT
___ Go there and work hard for the charity.
___ Get your photo taken without any disruption to the event.
___ Politely and friendly answer questions as to why you are getting your picture taken.
___ Develop new friendships from the inquisitive people that ask you questions.
___ Have fun!

Step 3. AFTER THE EVENT
___ Follow up with the organizer. Thank them for the invitation.
___ Discuss the idea of you helping them in the future through your acting career.
___ Do they need a spokesperson?
___ Follow up with anyone that you connected with at the event.
___ Create a press release of you wanting to give back to your community.

Creating your Own Marketing Postcards

___ Your contact information (but not your personal address).

___ Full body, the quarter-body shot and a headshot.

___ Designed around an event or genre.

___ Potentially use it as a press release.

___ Communicate a short message without being overwhelming.

___ Make it compelling.

___ Send them to fans about upcoming roles.

___ Send them to agents and managers that you want to sign with.

___ Use them as invitations to upcoming events.

___ Do not use preprinted labels. Handwrite every address if you mail them.

___ Continually update your mailing list.

___ If you are going to use someone else's likeness or logo, make sure that you have permission.

___ Make sure the handout/postcard is a standard mailing size.

___ If you want to print in small quantities, use one of the large drug store photo programs.

___ Send postcards out about every two months.

___ Clean and simple is always your best option.

___ DO NOT send out information on an upcoming project if you do not have the clearance yet.

___ Keep it professional.

___ ALWAYS, ALWAYS, ALWAYS make yourself look good!

ACTOR REEL
Check List

It must be around two minutes.

Remember, your actor reel is a video display of you performing your craft.

Filming

___ Cut scenes from a project you are in.

___ Tweak the sound, contrast and all of the other fun things.

Lighting

___ Choose (or make) a scene that provides you in a good light.

Sound

___ Make it sound fantastic, or do not use it.

Overall Appeal

___ Make it great.

___ Use clear text.

MAKE IT PROFRESSIONAL!!!

YOUR TEAM
Check List

Talent Agents
___ Stay in touch.
___ Check your email several times a day (that you set up just for casting notices) for messages
   from them.
___ Keep them updated with any physical changes (hair, weight, etc.).

Talent Managers
___ Develop your career plan with them.
___ Stay in touch.
___ How are they going to market you?
___ Are they helping you develop your brand?

Megaphone Team
Who are the members and what are their responsibilities?
1. _____
2. _____
3. _____

Social Media Influencers
Columnists –
Show Hosts –
Bloggers / Vloggers –
YouTube Hosts –
Stay in touch with them!

Crew for Headshots, Website, Filming Auditions and Editing Actor Reels
Web Site Guru –
Photographer –
Film Editor –
Stay in touch!

Fans
___ Find fun ways to connect with them.
___ Find ways to get them to spread the word about you.
___ Make sure that they understand your brand.

HAND OUT YOUR FACE
Check List

Hand Out Your Face Attitude
This is your career. This is your brand. This is your business. This is YOU!
___ YOU have to go out there and make this work.
___ YOU have got to lead your team to help you be more successful.
___ YOU have got to be the driving force behind your success.
___ YOU have got to believe in yourself.
___ YOU have got to know YOU are worth the recognition.
___ YOU have got to know that you are good enough.
___ YOU have got to know that you are worthy.
___ YOU have got to stay focused.
___ YOU must persevere!

Headshots
___ It should be a shoulders shot.
___ Your shoulders should be squared.
___ The camera should be level with your eyes.
___ Don't have your hands on your face.
___ Try to get the reflection of the lights in your eyes.
___ It should be simple and straightforward.
___ Your expressions should be subtle.
___ NEVER EVER touchup your headshot.
___ Keep a supply of your headshots with resumes on the back readily available.
___ Have several headshots made up. Let them portray your look in different ways.
___ Obviously, if you do anything to alter your look…get new shots.
___ Get a list of 6 to 8 casting directors that you would like to work with. Develop a cover letter.
___ Get a list of 6 to 8 filmmakers that you would like to work with. Develop a cover letter
___ Send them out every six months (if you do not have an agent).

Resume

List:
- ___ Your successes
- ___ Production companies you have worked with
- ___ Characters you've played
- ___ Directors and producers you've worked with
- ___ Teachers you've had
- ___ Special skills
- ___ Credits that stand out
  (A guest star role on a network show carries more weight than one on an unknown web series)
- ___ Keep your resume crisp and clean so that our eyes go straight to the most important details.
- ___ Put your credits by and large in chronological order.
- ___ If you do not yet have any impressive credits, focus on training that you have had.

KEEP IT UP TO DATE. KEEP IT UP TO DATE. KEEP IT UP TO DATE.

Business Cards

- ___ Give out "X" amount of cards to key people
- ___ MUST look professional
- ___ MUST impress the person receiving it
- ___ MUST be well-designed
- ___ MUST have your picture on it
- ___ Keep them on you
- ___ Give your elevator speech and hand them a card

PRESS RELEASE LINKS

Some of these are free. For some there is a charge. Be sure to check how long it

takes to get your Press Release listed.

This is just a list of links. This is not an endorsement of any link over another.

Be aware that links are subject to change.

121pressrelease.com	news.wooeb.com
1888PressRelease.com	onlineprnews.com
24-7PressRelease.com	openpr.com
25pressreleases.com	postafreepressrelease.com
articleshub.org	pr-canada.net
bignews.biz	PR-Inside.com
briefingwire.com	pr-gb.com
calameo.com	pr-usa.net
ClickPress.com	pr4links.com
del.icio.us	PR9.net
docstoc.com	PR.com
EcommWire.com	PRBuzz.com
exactrelease.com	PRCompass.com
Express-Press-Release.com	PRLeap.com
express-press-release.net	PRLog.org
forpressrelease.com	Press-Base.com
freebusinesswire.com	PressAbout.com
free-news-distribution.com	pressbooth.org
freepressrelease.com.au	pressbox.com
free-press-release.com	pressexposure.com
Free-Press-Release-Center.info	PressMethod.com
ideamarketers.com	pressreleaseforum.com
I-Newswire.com	pressreleasesfree.com
information-online.com	pressreleasepoint.com
jkhanok.com	PRUrgent.com
live-pr.com	scribd.com
malebits.com	seenation.com
mediasyndicate.com	stumbleupon.com
mynewssplash.com	submitfreepr.com
newsalbum.com	theopenpress.com
netforcepress.com	timinternet.com
newsbycompany.com	ukprwire.com
newdesignworld.com	usprwire.com
newpressrelease.com	webnewswire.com
NewswireToday.com	

PRESS RELEASE SAMPLE LAYOUTS

Eastern NC Film Festival
PO Box 1323
Winterville, NC 28590
(252) 367-8789

For More Information
John Doe
(212) 321-1000
bob@iamdoingitmyselfasanactor.com

FOR IMMEDIATE RELEASE/To Be Released on XX/XX/XX

Title

Location – Date – Summary news lead (who, what, where, when, why, how) and Benefit statement (who benefits?)

Info/action statement (where to get more information)

Secondary details (expand on first paragraph)

###

Actor Profile Directories

Actors & Extras | Talent Directory – www.starnow.com/Talent-Directory/United-States/Actors/

Actor Hub - Free Online Actor and Casting Call Directory - www.actorhub.com/

Spotlight - Professional acting jobs, auditions and castings - www.spotlight.com/

Players Directory - Actor Information - https://www.playersdirectory.com/info/actors.php

Actors and Actresses: Directories– Dmoz - http://www.dmoz.org/Arts/Performing_Arts/Acting/Actors_and_Actresses/

UK Talent Directory - www.castingnow.co.uk/talent-directory

The Page UK - A Casting directory for professional actors - https://www.thepageuk.com/

Backstage Resources - Call Sheet Database for Agents - www.backstage.com/resources/

CastNet - The UK Casting Agents resource for Castin - https://www.castnet.co.uk/

Ireland Actors Guide - irelandactorsguide.ie/

Extras - www.extras.com/

CONCLUSION

So there you have it.

I am not claiming that this book provides you with everything that you will ever need to market your career.

I am saying…it is a start.

I hope that you found all of this information helpful.

I hope that it has raised questions. That you will find the answers to making your career a success.

I even hope that it motivated you to take your career to the next level.

When it comes to your fans…create your brand, and then give your fans what you have created. Interact with them. Make it enjoyable to be your fan. Make it an experience. Make it where everyone wants to be…in your fan club.

How do you do that?

I don't know….It is your brand.

I truly want you to succeed. Be blessed, and break a leg!

Be sure you make the world a better place than you found it.

If I can answer any questions, you need a speaker for an event, or you are looking for a great talent manager…here is my contact info:

Ron Cooper
Kaleigh Group Entertainment
www.kaleighgroupentertainment.com
roncooper@kaleighgroupentertainment.com

Property of Kaleigh Group Media

No reproduction of this material without the express written consent of Ron Cooper or Kaleigh Group Media

Made in the USA
Lexington, KY
28 October 2015